GLOBETROTTER™

Travel Guide

ICELAND

Rowland Mead

D1056192

GLOBETROTTER™

★★★ Highly recommended
★★ Recommended
★ See if you can

Seventh edition published in 2015
by MapStudio™
10 9 8 7 6 5 4 3 2 1
www.globetrottertravelguides.com

Distributed in Africa by
MapStudio™
Unit 3, Block B, M5 Park, Eastman Road,
Maitland 7405, Cape Town, South Africa
PO Box 193, Maitland 7404

Distributed in the UK/Europe/Asia by
John Beaufoy Publishing Ltd

Distributed in the USA by
National Book Network

ISBN (Print) 978 1 77026 679 7
ISBN (ePdf) 978 1 77026 734 3

This guidebook has been written by independent authors and
updaters. The information therein represents their impartial
opinion, and neither they nor the publishers accept payment
in return for including in the book or writing more favourable
reviews of any of the establishments. Whilst every effort has
been made to ensure that this guidebook is as accurate and
up to date as possible, please be aware that the facts quoted
are subject to change, particularly the price of food, transport
and accommodation. The Publisher accepts no responsibility
or liability for any loss, injury or inconvenience incurred by
readers or travellers using this guide.

Commissioning Editor: Elaine Fick
DTP Cartographic Manager: Genené Hart
Editors: Elaine Fick, Thea Grobbelaar, Lorissa Bouwer, Nicky
Steenkamp, Melany Porter, Donald Reid
Cartographers: Rudi de Lange, Nicole Bannister, Inga
Ndibongo, Tanja Spinola, Marlon Christmas
Design and DTP: Nicole Bannister, Éloïse Moss
Picture Researcher: Shavonne Govender
Consultant: Richard Sale
Updated in 2015 by: Richard Sale

Reproduction by Hirt & Carter (Pty) Ltd, Cape Town
Printed and bound by Craft Print International Ltd, Singapore

Keep us current
Information in travel guides is apt to change, which is why
we regularly update our guides. We'd be grateful to receive
feedback if you've noted something we should include in
our updates. If you have new information, please share
it with us by writing to the Commissioning Editor at the
MapStudio address on this page. The most significant
contribution to each new edition will receive a free copy of
the updated guide.

Front Cover: *Skógafoss waterfall in winter.*
Title Page: *Turf houses at Skaftafell National Park.*

CONTENTS

1
Introducing Iceland

Over the last two decades, Iceland has become one of the world's fastest growing tourist destinations. The reasons are easy to appreciate. First, and above all, is the scenery. A volcanically active zone runs through the country from northeast to southwest following a tectonic plate boundary. Active **volcanoes** such as Hekla and Krafla have reared above lava plains and **geothermal areas**, which include geysers, fumeroles, hot springs and mud springs. There are numerous **icecaps**, including Vatnajökull, which is bigger than the rest of Europe's icecaps put together. **Glacier** tongues flow from the icecaps, with icebergs calving from their snouts, sometimes into glacial lagoons, such as that at Jökulsárlón. Steep-sided **fiords**, formed by glaciers, punctuate the northwest and south-east coast, giving shelter for fishing villages. Iceland even has **deserts** – in this case the cold variety. In fact, because of the icecaps, lava fields and deserts, over 70% of the country is uninhabitable.

Iceland has a population of just under 325,600 (1 Jan 2014 estimate), of which about 55% live in '**greater Reykjavík**' (**the capital, Kópavogur and Hafnarfjörður**). As well as being one of the least crowded countries in the world (less than a million people have lived in Iceland since the first settlement), it is also one of the least polluted – all its power is from geothermal sources – and the clear light will delight photographers. The country is a **bird-watcher's joy**, with teeming 'sea-bird cities' on its cliffs and abundant wildfowl on lakes such as Mývatn. Others come to Iceland for **outdoor activities** – hiking, white-water rafting or snowmobile rides across an icecap. But do not

TOP ATTRACTIONS

*** **Lake Mývatn:** great range of birds and some fascinating volcanic features.
*** **Geysir Area:** geysers and other geothermal surprises; Gullfoss waterfall and Skáholt Cathedral.
*** **Jökulsárlón:** boat trip on a glacial lagoon amongst melting icebergs.
*** **Hallgrímskirkja:** modern church with superb views over the rooftops of Reykjavík.
*** **Þingvellir:** lakeside site of ancient parliament.
*** **Blue Lagoon:** hot-water swimming pools alongside a geothermal power station.

◄ *Opposite: A snowy scene at Þingvellir, the site of Iceland's parliament.*

INTRODUCING ICELAND

▲ *Above: A distant view of Vatnajökull, Iceland's largest icecap.*

FACTS AND FIGURES

- **Size**: It covers 102,819km² (39,688 sq miles), making it the second largest island in Europe. Its greatest distance from north to south is 300km (186 miles) and from east to west 500km (310 miles).
- **Position**: Lies between latitude 63°N and 66°N and longitude 13°W and 24°W.
- **Population**: 325,600 (2014), concentrated in the southwest. Population density is 3.1/km².
- **Land Use**: Only 12,000km² (4632 sq miles) is farmed.
- **Religion**: 97% claim to be Lutheran Protestants.
- **Highest mountain**: Hvannadalshnjúkur at 2119m (6952ft).
- **Longest river**: Þjórsá at 237km (147 miles).

come here for sun-drenched beaches, as they are composed of black volcanic sand and pounded by massive Atlantic waves.

THE LAND

Situated in the North Atlantic Ocean, just south of the Arctic Circle (the Circle passes through the island of Grimsey off the northern coast), Iceland covers just over 100,000km² (38,600 sq miles), making it the second largest island in Europe. The nearest land masses are Greenland – 287km (178 miles) to the northwest; Norway – 970km (603 miles) to the east; and Scotland – 798km (496 miles) to the southeast. Iceland is the largest of a series of islands positioned on the submarine mountain chain known as the Mid-Atlantic Ridge, which marks a **plate boundary** separating the American Plate from the Eurasian Plate, which are moving apart at an average rate of 1–2cm (½–1 in) a year. Geologists delight in stating that the west of Iceland is in North America and the east of the country is in Europe! It is also true that, geologically speaking, Iceland is the youngest country in Europe.

The **volcanic belt** runs in a northeasterly direction, from the southwest of the country in the Reykanes Peninsula area towards Lake Mývatn in the northeast. It varies in width from 40km (25 miles) to 60km (37 miles) and is typified by volcanoes and other forms of volcanic activity such as geysers, hot springs, mud springs, fumeroles and solfataras. The majority of the lava is of the scoria type, which is coarse, loose and sharp and which often solidifies into fantastic shapes. Volcanic activity has continued throughout recorded history, with the most recent eruptions being at Surtsey in 1963, Heimaey in 1973, Krafla in the mid-70s and Hekla in 1991, while in 2010 Eyjafjallajökull produced an ash cloud which grounded most of Europe's planes for over a week and played havoc with many people's travel plans. An eruption of the Bárðarbunga volcano in 2014 was more powerful, but caused no large ash cloud. In the east and west of Iceland, away from the active volcanic zone, are mountains of basalt and rhyolite, the result of lava flows up to 20 million years ago.

Being on a plate boundary, Iceland often experiences **earthquakes**, the latest in May 2008 which recorded 6.3 on the Richter scale. The quake's epicentre was near Selfoss and although there was damage to property, there were no fatalities. Several earthquakes of 5+ on the scale accompanied the 2014 Bárðarbunga eruption.

Another important feature in the shaping of Iceland is **ice**. The country is still in the throes of the Ice Age and enormous icecaps can be seen where the land is about 1300m (4265ft) above sea level. The biggest icecap is **Vatnajökull**, the largest in Europe and also the world's third greatest after Antarctica and Greenland. Tongues of ice, called valley **glaciers**, spread out from the icecaps, eroding deep U-shaped valleys and creating a number of spectacular **fiords**. The material eroded by the glaciers is eventually deposited on outwash plains or

PLATE TECTONICS

The modern science of Plate Tectonics has its origins in the work of **Alfred Wegener**, who in 1912 published his work on **Continental Drift**. It was rejected then as he did not suggest a mechanism by which this drift could occur. It is now known that convection currents can move plates in various ways, causing three types of margin:
Constructive Margins, with plates moving apart and volcanic material forming new land (as in the case of the Mid-Atlantic Ridge in Iceland);
Destructive Margins, with plates moving together to form fold mountains; and
Passive Margins, where plates move sideways, causing earthquake activity.

▼ *Below: Lingering snow in the Landmannalaugar area on one of the main routes through the interior.*

INTRODUCING ICELAND

Volcanoes are mountains formed when hot molten lava is forced through weak points in the earth's crust. The material may be liquid, as in the case of **lava**, or solid, as with volcanic **bombs** or **ash**. Steam and gases are also commonly found around volcanoes. Volcanoes generally have a distinct **crater**, which may fill with rain water to form a **crater lake**. The shape of a volcano depends very much on the type of material erupted. The most common volcanic material seen in Iceland is **basalt**, which is a very fluid lava, forming extensive **lava fields**. Those volcanoes which are erupting at present are known as **active**, while those which are totally dead are called **extinct**. Volcanoes which are temporarily quiet are said to be **dormant**.

sandur – lowland areas covered with sand, gravel and braided streams. The largest of the sandur is Skeiðarársandur, situated to the south of the Vatnajökull icecap. The juxtaposition of ice and volcanic activity can have calamitous effects, such as the *jökulhlaup*, where volcanic activity under an icecap melts the ice to cause huge amounts of glacial flood water.

Mountains and Rivers

Many of Iceland's **rivers** have their sources on the icecaps, particularly on Vatnajökull. The Skjálfandafljót and the Jökulsá á Fjöllum flow northwards to reach the sea to the west and east of Húsavík, while the Lagarfljót runs northeast through Egilsstaðir on its route to the Atlantic. The main river of the southwest is the Þjórsá, which rises in the interior and arrives at the sea east of Selfoss. The volume of water in Iceland's rivers gives rise to some spectacular **waterfalls**, including Gullfoss, east of Reykjavík, or the magnificent Dettifoss in the northeast. Iceland's highest **mountains** are called **nunataks**, or mountains which rise above the level of the ice. They include Hvannadalshnjúkur, at 2119m (6952ft), and Barðarbunga, at 2009m (6592ft), both on Vatnajökull. Just as spectacular, although not necessarily as high, are Iceland's volcanoes – particularly Hekla, at 1491m (4892ft), which has a perfect cone shape, capped by snow and ice.

Geology

Seas and Shores

The hard, volcanic rocks of Iceland have produced some truly majestic **cliffs**, alive with nesting sea birds in the summer. Winds, particularly those from the prevailing southwest, whip up strong waves which erode the cliffs into **sea stacks** and **arches**, such as those at Dyrhólaey, near Vík. In other areas, deep **fiords** provide safe harbours for fishing fleets. Less common are **spits** – these are long ridges of sand and shingle formed by longshore drift and marine deposition. They are best seen to the east and west of Höfn, where a narrow gap in the spit leads to a sheltered harbour.

Climate

Iceland's maritime climate is noted in particular for its changeability. The people of Iceland are fond of saying, 'if you don't like the weather right now, just wait a few moments and it will change'. Weather conditions such as wind, rain, snow, hail and fog can all feature within a single day, so visitors to this destination need to be prepared for all eventualities.

Iceland's geographical position directly in the path of the **Gulf Stream** combined with the prevailing westerly winds means that winters here are milder than in cities of a more southerly latitude such as Toronto, New York and Moscow. The downside is that though they are less harsh, the winters can be extremely wet, particularly in the south-western parts of the country around Reykjavík, where the wind makes the climate even more miserable. The situation barely improves in summer, when the capital receives on average only one fine day during the month of July.

▲ *Above: The Atlantic waves attack the steep cliffs of basalt at Krýsuvíkurberg on the Reykjanes Peninsula.*

TUNDRA AND PERMAFROST

The higher parts of the interior of Iceland have an ecosystem known as the **tundra**. This is a result of the long, severe winters, a short growing season and precipitation which falls mainly as snow. The ground is permanently frozen, apart from the top 50cm (20in) or so which melts in summer. This condition is known as permafrost. Because of the **permafrost**, the surface of the land is often marshy and badly drained in the summer.

COMPARATIVE CLIMATE CHART	REYKJAVÍK				AKUREYRI				EGILSSTAÐIR			
	WIN	SPR	SUM	AUT	WIN	SPR	SUM	AUT	WIN	SPR	SUM	AUT
	JAN	APR	JULY	OCT	JAN	APR	JULY	OCT	JAN	APR	JULY	OCT
AVERAGE TEMP. ºC	-0.8	2	11	5	-1.8	3.5	11	3.9	-1.3	1.4	9.9	4.5
AVERAGE TEMP. ºF	30.5	35.6	51.8	41	28.7	38.3	51.8	39	29.6	34.5	49.8	40
RAINFALL mm	76	58	52	86	55	29	33	58	134	87	97	169
RAINFALL in	3	2.3	2	3.4	2.1	1.1	1.3	2.3	5.3	3.4	3.8	6.7
DAYS OF RAINFALL	19	17	15	19	16	12	12	17	20	16	15	20

INTRODUCING ICELAND

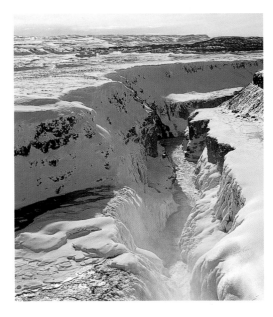

▲ *Above: The mighty Gullfoss waterfall may be almost completely frozen in winter.*

LAND OF THE MIDNIGHT SUN

This is a descriptive title which is often applied to Iceland, but it is only partly true. It never really gets dark anywhere in Iceland during June, but to actually be able to see the sun at midnight means going to a location within the Arctic Circle. The only place where this is possible is on the island of Grímsey, about 41km (25 miles) north of Akureyri. Unfortunately for Grimsey, it sees no sun at all during the month of January.

The more eastern and northern fringes of the country, which are in the rain shadow of the central mountains and icecaps, fare rather better from the point of view of sunshine. Akureyri, in the north, is the warmest part of the country and Egilsstaðir, in the east, is the driest. When the wind blows from the Arctic, however, the temperature can drop alarmingly. Fogs are common on the eastern side of the country, particularly when cold ocean currents from the north meet the more temperate Gulf Stream. Snowfall is heavy in the interior of the country, especially on the high icecaps. Much of the interior is only free enough of snow to allow transport during the months of July and August. In the drier cold deserts and sandur, windblown dust and gravel can seriously damage the paintwork of vehicles and make a misery of a cycling holiday. Visitors, however, will also remember Iceland for its clarity of light, largely thanks to the unpolluted environment.

Iceland's position close to the Arctic Circle means that its daylight hours vary considerably between summer and winter. During the winter months of December and January, three to four hours of daylight are as much as can be expected, and Icelanders can suffer from 'short-day depression', with suicide rates increasing at this time of the year. One compensation, however, is that this is the best season to see the *aurora borealis*, or Northern Lights. The situation is reversed in the summer, when in June and July daylight continues throughout the night.

Wildlife

One of the main characteristics of the fauna and flora of Iceland is the small number of species to be seen. There are obvious reasons for this – until the end of the Ice Age some 20,000 years ago, Iceland was covered with snow and glaciers. With the climate improving only slowly, the recolonization of plants and animals has been a gradual process, and even today the inhospitable climate and the short growing season are limiting factors. A further reason is the fact that Iceland is an island in an isolated part of the North Atlantic Ocean, making the migration of species difficult.

The only **mammal** which is indigenous to Iceland is the **arctic fox**. Farmers have always blamed the fox for killing lambs, and large numbers have been shot. In fact, the arctic fox lives mainly on small birds and rodents, although it is also a scavenger and can be seen finishing off carcasses of sea birds or sheep. The arctic fox changes the colour of its coat in winter, and a small minority of the species turns completely white. Numbers of arctic foxes have dropped considerably and visitors will be lucky to see this wary animal.

There have been a number of mammals **introduced** inadvertently, particularly rodents. **Reindeer** were brought in from Norway in the 18th century, but as Icelanders did not readily take to the idea of living as nomadic reindeer herders, the animals reverted to the wild. They were often hunted, both for meat and to prevent them grazing valuable sheep pastures, so that their numbers have frequently dropped to dangerously low levels. The reindeer is now a protected species in Iceland,

▼ Below: The arctic fox, Iceland's only indigenous mammal, is wary of man.

INTRODUCING ICELAND

and they live in scattered groups, mainly in the east of the country. **American mink** were introduced for fur farming in the 1930s, and escaped mink can be found throughout the country in marine and freshwater sites. **Polar bears** from Greenland occasionally reach Iceland on ice floes.

Marine mammals are much more plentiful, with around 20 species regularly visiting Icelandic waters. Both common (or harbour) and grey **seals** breed around the coast, and Iceland has around half the world's total population of common seals – the best time to see them is at the end of June when they are pupping. **Walruses** also occasionally appear, mainly on the northwest coast. Spring and summer are the best times to see **whales**. Since the killing of whales has been banned, a number of Icelandic fishing ports have begun to specialize in whale-watching trips which have proved popular with visitors. The most commonly seen whales are sperm, minke, killer and fin, while common **porpoises** and white-beaked **dolphins** also turn up. Iceland's decision in late 2003 to resume a limited amount of whaling for 'scientific purposes' has roused huge international criticism.

There is no doubt that it is the **birds** which comprise the most spectacular part of Iceland's fauna. Although there are only around 70 resident breeding bird species, there are a large number of migrants and accidental visitors, making the Iceland list top well over 300 species. What attracts birders to the country is the rarity of the birds and the fact that they are a curious mixture of European, North American, Arctic and temperate species – three North American species (Barrow's goldeneye, the great northern diver and the harlequin duck), for example, are found nowhere else in Europe.

▼ *Below: Since the banning of whaling, orcas or killer whales have become increasingly common in Icelandic waters.*

Sea birds breed in incredible numbers and include gulls, guillemots, skuas, puffins, razorbills, gannets, kittiwakes, fulmars, shags and cormorants. Iceland has an abundance of wetland sites which provide the ideal breeding habitat for geese, whooper swans and a wide variety of ducks. The most important breeding site is Lake Mývatn, where there are vast numbers of tufted duck, scaup, mallard, pintail, gadwall, wigeon and teal. Wading birds, too, are well represented, though birds of prey are limited to the merlin, the gyrfalcon, the threatened white-tailed sea eagle, and the rare snowy owl.

Iceland's freshwater areas abound with **fish**, but there are only five main varieties: Arctic char, eels, salmon, trout and sticklebacks. Visitors should be aware that licences for salmon fishing are cripplingly expensive. On the other hand, there is a rich variety of **oceanic fish**, including cod, haddock, whiting, plaice, ling, sole, redfish and herring. Of the larger fish, the Greenland shark is common in Iceland, and its meat is a popular delicacy.

Iceland's geographical isolation has meant that certain types of fauna are missing. No butterflies breed, although certain migrants, such as painted ladies, may appear in some years. Iceland has no amphibians, such as frogs, toads and newts. Nor, visitors will be pleased to know, are there any snakes!

▲ Above left: An eider duck's nest, showing the down that is collected for use in bedding.
▲ Above right: The fulmar is Iceland's most common seabird, often nesting on inland cliffs.

BIRDS YOU WILL NOT SEE

The climate and the natural vegetation of Iceland have a limiting effect on the range of birds to be seen. The lack of mature trees means that many of the **passerine** (perching) birds, such as **warblers**, are missing. So are hole-nesting species such as **woodpeckers**, **nuthatches** and **treecreepers**. The general lack of insect life cuts out **swallows**, **martins** and **swifts**. Furthermore, the often frozen water prohibits **kingfishers**. Nor will you find **penguins** – they are confined to the Antarctic!

▲ *Above: A field of white cotton grass in a valley surrounded by sea and mountain.*
▶ *Opposite: Wild flowers are quick to colonize newly weathered soil on glacial moraine and lava flows.*

TUNDRA FLORA

Because of the permafrost conditions and the short growing season, plants on the tundra areas of Iceland have barely two months to complete their life cycles. Such plants must have a very high tolerance to cold and to lack of moisture (water is often unavailable as it is stored as snow or ice). Not surprisingly there are fewer species of plants on the tundra than on any other biome. Plants which do survive tend to be low-growing and rounded in order to gain protection from the wind. Flowering plants can be spectacular, with 'bloom mats' of anenomes, arctic poppies, saxifrages and gentians.

Flora

One of the first things that visitors notice about Iceland is the scarcity of **trees**. For much of the country, dwarf and scrubby willow and birch are the best that can be seen. It is claimed that early inhabitants felled the trees for building materials and fuel, and that sheep prevented regeneration by eating new shoots. Not everyone agrees with this opinion, however, as the Old Norse word for 'woods' is the same as the present-day word for 'willows'. Could it be that the widespread 'forests' were little more than the same scrub seen today? There are two areas of impressive woodland near Hallormssta∂arskógur in the east of the country and at Fnjóskadalur in the north. Many surburban gardens in Reykjavík, helped by a climatic 'heat island', also have a good collection of small trees.

The range of **flowering plants** is small but of considerable interest. It is largely of North European character. Early in the summer cushions of moss campion abound, particularly on the mature lava flows. Dandelions and Alaska lupins are also common at this time of the year, while later in the year vast swathes of white cotton grass cover the landscape. On the heathlands and moorlands, low-growing shrubs are dominant and include whortleberry, crowberry and bearberry. Mosses and lichens are found everywhere and are usually the first plants to colonize new lava flows. Geothermal regions develop their own assemblage of heat-loving plants.

HISTORICAL CALENDAR

700s Irish monks in Iceland.

800s Norse colonization of Iceland begins.

870 The first recognized settler, Ingólfur Arnarson, sets up home in the Reykjavík area.

930 The population reaches around 60,000. Immigrants are mainly people dissatisfied with life in Norway. The Alþing (National Assembly) is set up near Þingvellir Lake.

930–1230 The Saga Age.

990 Leifur Eiríksson discovers North America.

1106 Bishoprics are established at Skálholt and Hólar.

1220 Beginning of the Sturling Period, marked by feuds and violence.

1241 Sturluson is murdered.

1262 Iceland comes under the Norwegian crown.

1300s Period of disasters – earthquakes, volcanic eruptions, famines and diseases.

1397 Iceland and Norway under the Danish crown.

1550 Reformation imposed by the Danish king. The last Catholic bishop is beheaded.

1700s More volcanic activity, including, in 1783, the Laki eruption. The ash cloud raised by the eruption blocked out the sun for three years, the 'Haze of Hunger' as it is now called, led to crop failures and widespread famine.

1798 The Alþing moves from Þingvellir to Reykjavík.

1840s Campaign for self-rule led by Jón Sigurdsson.

1904 Home rule is achieved under Danish control.

1940 Denmark occupied by Germany. The Alþing decides that the union with Denmark is now void. Iceland is occupied by British troops as a strategic defence measure.

1941 The USA takes over the defence of Iceland and establishes a base at Keflavík.

1944 Iceland declared an independent republic at Þingvellir on 17 June.

1946 Iceland joins United Nations Organization.

1949 Iceland becomes a founding member of NATO.

1958 The first of the so-called 'Cod Wars' with Britain over fishery rights.

1970 Iceland joins EFTA.

1974 Iceland's 1406km (874-mile) Ring Road is completed.

1980 Vigdís Finnbogadóttir becomes the world's first democratically elected woman President.

1986 Reagan–Gorbachov summit held at Reykjavík.

1989 Iceland ceases commercial whaling.

1990s Tourism begins to develop as a major foreign currency earner.

2003 Limited whaling resumed for 'scientific reasons'.

2008 World economic recession hits Iceland badly. Its stock market crashes and its three main banks go into receivership.

2009 Iceland applied for EU membership, but in 2013 withdrew its application.

2010 An ash cloud from the volcano Eyjafjallajökull paralyses northern European air travel.

2014 Bárðarbunga eruption.

HISTORY IN BRIEF

Iceland's first recorded inhabitants were Irish monks who came to the area, probably by sea-going coracles, in the 700s. They had fled persecution in their own country and came to Iceland seeking a life of quiet contemplation. These hermits fled when the first Norse settlers came around the year 870. The first known Norseman to reach Icelandic shores was a Viking called

INTRODUCING ICELAND

▶ *Opposite: The 19th-century wooden church at Þingvellir.*
▼ *Below: Statue of Leifur Eiríksson, who is believed to have discovered North America in 990.*

Naddodur. He found an unpromising snowy landscape. He called the country 'Snæland' and immediately sailed away. Later, a Swede called Garðar Svavarsson circumnavigated the land, confirming that it was an island. In 860, a third Viking called Flóki Vilgerðson navigated his way to the country with the aid of three ravens. He landed in the Breiðafjörður area, where his party spent the winter. He had neglected, however, to collect enough hay for winter food for his animals, which then perished. He named the island 'Iceland' and returned to Norway.

The settlement of Iceland now gathered pace. The immigrants were mainly from Norway where they were disenchanted with the tyrranical rule of King Harald Fair-hair. It is officially recognized that the first permanent settler was **Ingólfur Arnarson**, who arrived in 874. It is said that Arnarson selected the spot where they put ashore in the traditional Viking way by throwing his high seat pillar overboard and waiting to see where it landed. Arnarson named the area Reykjavík (smoky bay) after the vapours from the local hot springs.

Early Government

The period of settlement was over by 930, when the population had reached around 25,000. Arnarson's son, Þorsteinn Ingólfsson, founded the first 'Þing', or local assembly, and in 930 he was one of the founder members of the **Alþing** or general assembly. The assembly was needed because a number of self-ruling groups had sprung up around the country and a code of law became necessary. The site of the Alþing was chosen to be on the shores of Lake Þingvellir, where delegates came from all over the country for two weeks every year. New laws were decreed, judgements were passed, criminals were punished and claims settled. The opportunity was also taken for marriages to be arranged and business deals to be concluded. For this purpose, a number of stone booths were erected and the remains of these can still be seen today. The Assembly also elected the influential law-speaker, whose task was to recite from memory one third of the country's laws each year. Around the year 1000, the Alþing decreed that Iceland should be a **Christian** rather than a pagan country. Although generally peaceful, there were times when the Alþing degenerated into chaos as armed groups took justice into their own hands and pitched battles resulted.

The Middle Ages

Violence escalated in the mid-13th century, which became known as the **Sturlung Period**. There were ferocious power struggles between the more influential families, the most significant of which were the descendants of Sturla. A key figure at this time was **Snorri Sturluson**, a writer and diplomat. He eventually fell foul of the Norwegian King Hákon the Old, who ordered Snorri's death. In the ensuing chaos, Hákon took over, and by 1262, the Icelanders were forced to surrender their independence to Norway.

The 14th century was an unhappy time for Icelanders, with social hardship and a string of natural catastrophes. Hekla erupted several times and the Black Death reached Iceland, killing two-thirds of the population. In 1380, both Norway and Iceland came under the rule of Denmark, follow-ing the Kalmar Union. The Danes imposed the Reformation and Lutheranism on the country and, when the Catholic Bishop of Hólar resisted the changes, he and his two sons were summarily beheaded. In 1602, Denmark introduced a trade monopoly granting exclusive trading rights in Iceland to Danish and Swedish firms. The woes of the Icelanders continued into the 18th century, when a smallpox outbreak killed a third of the population. There were also frequent natural disasters, with the eruptions of Hekla and Katla both leading to widespread famine. The most cataclysmic disaster, however, was the eruption, in 1783, of Laki. This went on for

THE SAGAS

The age of the Sagas was from the late 12th to the late 13th centuries. They were epic stories, written largely anonymously, about the early settlers and their struggle to survive. Human relationships were described in detail, so they contain much accurate historical information, including the violent battles and family feuds of the time. The Sagas were often recited by a member of the family while the others worked. They provided entertainment during the boredom of the cold winter nights. The Sagas were written in old Norse and because of the isolation of Iceland, the language has changed little over the centuries, enabling Icelanders today to read the transcribed accounts. Around 40 Sagas were written. The best known is the *Egils Saga*, the biography of Egill Skallagrísson, while the most popular, because of the sympathetic characters, is the *Njáls Saga*.

ten months, creating the largest lava field of historical times and producing a poisonous haze which destroyed pasture, crops and 75% of the country's livestock. The resulting famine killed nearly 20% of the population.

THE ICELANDIC MANUSCRIPTS

The Sagas and the other historical manuscripts of Iceland were originally written on vellum. When printing was developed in the 16th century, the old parchments lost their significance and many were lost. At the beginning of the 18th century, Árni Magnusson, a lecturer at Copenhagen University, made it his life's work to collect as many Icelandic manuscripts as he could find. Some were destroyed by fire in Copenhagen in 1728, but those that survivied were bequeathed to the University of Copenhagen. After independence in 1944, the people naturally wanted their manuscripts back. The Danish parliament authorized this in 1965 and the first batch arrived back in Iceland six years later. The complete collection is now housed in the Árni Magnusson Institute, which is part of the University of Reykjavík.

Towards Independence

From this low point in Iceland's history, things could only get better, and the 19th century saw the beginnings of the movement towards **independence**. The Alþing, which had been abolished by Denmark, was partially restored in Reykjavík. Denmark then lifted the trade restrictions in 1854 and the freedom of the press followed a year later. An important figure at this time was **Jón Sigurðsson**, a scholar and politician, who lobbied for the restoration of free trade and a return to the full powers of the Alþing. In 1874, Iceland was given its own constitution and was at last able to handle its own financial matters. In 1918, Denmark recognized Iceland as an independent state, although still within the Kingdom of Denmark, which retained responsibility for defence and foreign affairs. When Germany occupied Denmark in 1940, Iceland took control of its own affairs, requesting complete independence.

World War II was now raging and British troops occupied Iceland, which had no armed forces and would be vulnerable to German attack. In 1941, US forces took over and stayed on after the war, when the main threat came from Russia. On 17 June 1944, Iceland declared itself an **independent republic**. Thousands of Icelanders went to Þingvellir, the site of the original parliament, to celebrate the event.

The Modern Era

In the postwar years, Iceland's international participation grew apace when it joined the United Nations, and then in 1949 became one of the founder members of NATO. Iceland also maintained its traditional ties with its Nordic neighbours by becoming part of the Nordic Council.

In 1958 Iceland extended its fishery limits to 20km (12 miles), provoking the first of the **Cod Wars** with Britain. The second Cod War came in 1972, when the limit was extended to 75km (47 miles). The limit was then extended to 320km (200 miles) in 1975, leading to the third Cod War. When Iceland threatened to withdraw from NATO and break off diplomatic relations, Britain was forced to accept the limits. It was Iceland, however, which had to back down over the whaling issue, due to environmental pressure. At the moment the whaling industry in Iceland is dormant – being restricted to the culling of a number of minkes for 'scientific purposes'.

Iceland made considerable social advances in the postwar years. It was the first country in the world to have a woman president, and had a thriving Women's Party (which amalgamated with smaller parties in order to oppose the Independence Party). It has comprehensive health and education services, clean air and good housing. The unemployment rate is low and life expectancy is high. Today Iceland's living standards are amongst the highest in the world, but the country's stability was rocked in 2008, when the world economic crisis hit Iceland seriously, leading to the failure of the three main banks and the eventual collapse of the government. The incoming left-of-centre coalition administration stabilised the country, but in 2013 the old centre-right coalition, the grouping which had created the 2008 mess, was voted back in.

ECONOMIC COLLAPSE

With the world financial crisis in 2008, it became clear that Iceland's economy was built on unsustainable debt. Gordon Brown's anti-terrorist legislation froze the assets of Icesave, in which over 300,000 British people had invested. Despite help from the IMF, the standard of living in Iceland fell, leading to riots, protests and the fall of the government in January 2009. The replacement coalition led by Jóhanna Sigurðardóttir (the world's first openly gay prime minister) immediately applied for EU membership, with the hope of the euro replacing the króna in 2011. But the application was rescinded after the 2013 general election when Sigurðardóttir's coalition was replaced.

◄ Opposite: Crowds surround the statue of Jón Sigurðsson in Reykjavík on Iceland's National Day.
▼ Below: Iceland's fishing fleet has the benefit of a 330km exclusion zone.

INTRODUCING ICELAND

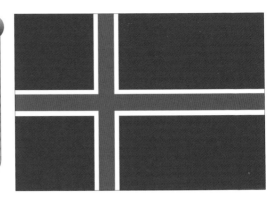

▲ *Above: Icelanders are exceedingly proud of their national flag, which is seen throughout the country, flying from prominent buildings as well as the most humble farmsteads.*

▼ *Below: A man and toddler celebrate the Icelandic National Day, which is typified by various parades, music and folk dancing.*

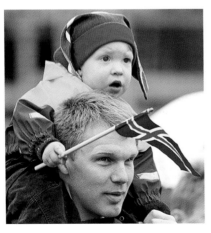

GOVERNMENT AND ECONOMY

Iceland has been an independent democratic republic since 1944 (although it could be argued that it is the world's oldest parliamentary democracy). The parliament, or Alþing, has 63 members, of whom around a third are usually women. The parliament is elected from eight constituencies for a four-year term. A system of proportional representation is used and every citizen has the right to vote and to stand for parliament. The main **political parties** are, on the right, the Independence Party and the Progressive Party, and, on the left, the Social Democratic Alliance and the Left-Green Movement. The distribution of votes inevitably means that Iceland has a **coalition government**, currently a centre-right alliance led by Sigmundur Davíð Gunnlaugsson. Presidential elections take place on a four-year basis. The president has a largely ceremonial and figurehead role. The fifth president of Iceland, who has held office since 1996, being returned for a fifth term in 2102 is Ólafur Ragnar Grímsson. Local government is run on the basis of 23 administrative counties, or *syslur*, subdivided into 200 rural districts, or *hreppur*.

Defence

Iceland has no armed forces of its own apart from a few armed fishery protection and coast-guard vessels. Its security is guaranteed by its membership of NATO. The United States maintained a controversial naval air base at Keflavík from 1951 until September 2006, when it pulled out. The cessation of the Cold War with Russia made the base redundant (along with the 900 Icelanders who worked there). Communication equipment remains and the US has promised to continue to guarantee Iceland's security.

▲ *Above: Woolly Icelandic sheep are an important export of Iceland.*

The Economy

Iceland's economy relies heavily on **fishing**, which accounts for over 70% of the country's exports. There are over 900 vessels engaged in fishing, producing an annual catch of around 1.5 million tonnes. The fishing fleet, however, accounts for only 5% of the workforce, with a further 8% involved in fish processing. Fish are exported fresh, frozen, canned and salted. The main fish caught here are cod, redfish, capelin, haddock and saithe. Shellfish include prawns and lobster. Successful experiments have been carried out in salmon and trout farming. The traditional government opposition to joining the EU is primarily because of Icelanders' fear of losing control over their fishing resources.

Due to the short growing season and the brief, cool summer, only about 1% of the country is devoted to **farming**. Iceland is outside the northern limit of grain production, so the most important crop is hay, which is used as winter food for cattle and sheep. There are over half a million sheep in Iceland and lamb is an important export. In summer, the sheep graze in the highlands so that the better pastures can be used for hay. Farming has become increasingly mechanized and many of the boggy lowlands

FEMALE POLITICIANS

The president in Iceland has a figurehead role, much like that of a monarch in some other countries. In 1980, the Icelanders elected a woman, **Vigdís Finnbogadóttir**, as president. This was the first time that a woman had been democratically elected to the position of president anywhere in the Western World. A popular and respected president, Vigdís was re-elected for three further terms before she stepped down in 1996 to devote herself to other work. In 2009, Iceland's financial crisis led to the resignation of the prime minister. His successor – leader of the new coalition government – was a woman, Jóhanna Sigurðardóttir, who was the world's first openly gay prime minister.

▲ *Above: Geothermal plants supply energy for homes, industry and horticulture.*

SUMMER HOTELS

Iceland's short summer means a high demand for hotel accommodation from June to August. In most areas it would be uneconomical for hotels to stay open the rest of the year. Iceland has devised a unique solution. During the academic year many students board at schools and colleges, and the buildings can be turned into hotels for the vacation (late May to early September). When the students leave, working parties move in and transform the buildings with new furnishings and signs, and visitors seldom realize that the hotel had an educational function for the rest of the year. The college sports facilities and pools can be used by guests, while senior students can work in the hotels as waitresses and cleaners and earn some holiday cash.

have been drained. Nevertheless, the number of farm workers has dropped and rural areas have been depopulated as Icelanders increasingly prefer an urban environment. The remaining farmers have been encouraged to diversify and many make a supplementary living out of tourism by offering farmhouse accommodation. Cheap geothermal electricity has led to the growth of a greenhouse industry, specializing in the production of tomatoes and other salad crops. Flowers and tropical fruits such as bananas are also grown. The industry is centred around Hveragerði in the southwest of Iceland. Many people are employed in the production of both geothermal and hydroelectric energy, the low cost of which has encouraged the development of aluminium smelting and diatom production (*see* page 86).

The largest growth industry is **tourism**. It is currently increasing both its income and the number of tourists who visit the country by 4–5% a year – almost three-quarters of a million visitors annually. Accurate statistics are difficult to obtain, however, since many visitors are transit passengers en route to North America or Europe, while others are Icelanders returning from working abroad. The majority of visitors come to Iceland in the brief summer season from July to August, when there is considerable pressure on accommodation. To overcome this, many boarding schools and colleges are turned into hotels for this period.

Inflation has often been a problem in Iceland, although in the early years of the present century it was largely under control. All this was to change in 2008 with the world financial crisis, when it reached nearly 14%. **Unemployment** has traditionally been low, with many Icelanders having more than one job in order to maintain a decent standard of living, but the economic meltdown has increased unemployment to 5.5% (Oct 2014). Over half of Iceland's **exports** go to the Eurozone, with 14% coming to the UK. The main exports are fish and fish products, aluminium and alloys, and animal products. The main **imports** are machinery and equipment, petroleum products, foodstuffs and textiles.

THE PEOPLE

It is frequently claimed that Icelanders are, in origin, the 'least Nordic' of the Scandinavian people, with research showing that there is a significant Celtic element in their genes. However, the country does not have a history of absorbing foreigners. Even today, immigration is strictly controlled. Visitors are likely to find that Icelanders are shy upon a first encounter, but this reserve usually gives way to warm hospitality.

Icelandic Names

Most Icelanders have a **patronymic** rather than a family surname, a system which was once common throughout Scandinavia. It is usual for a father, mother, daughter and son each to have a different last name. It works like this: a child takes his father's first name for a surname, to which is added 'son' if the child is a boy or 'dóttir' if a girl. Their own first name is then added. But there are further complications, because a woman retains her own name on marriage. This means that with a family comprising husband, wife, son and daughter, each family member will have a different last name. For example, the father might be called Magnus Jónsson, the son Sigurdur Magnusson, the daughter Gudrún Magnusdottír and the wife Vígdis Kristjándottír. For these reasons, Icelanders always refer to each other by their first name and will expect visiting foreigners to do likewise.

COPING WITH THE TELEPHONE DIRECTORY

Hotel guests paging through a telephone directory to ring a business colleague or friend are in for a shock. Firstly, Iceland is such a small place that the whole country can be covered in one directory. Secondly, everyone is listed by their first names, rather than their surnames. This means that there might be three pages of entries under the name of, say, Leifur. After the Christian name and surname, the profession of the person is given, then the address. Thirdly, a husband and wife living at the same address and sharing a telephone will have separate entries – quite sensible really! Another useful feature is that many Icelanders also list their e-mail address in the directory.

▼ *Below: Icelandic children in traditional woollen hats. In the remote rural areas, children attend boarding school from an early age.*

INTRODUCING ICELAND

Language

The geographical isolation of Iceland has enabled the country to maintain a language which is similar to Old Norse. The language is closely linked to the culture of the country so that its preservation is a matter of national pride and identity. It has changed so little over time that Icelanders are still able to read the transcribed Sagas written over 700 years ago. Sometimes called the 'Latin of the North', Icelandic is a highly complex language and very difficult for non-Nordic people to learn. After mastering their own tongue, Icelanders tend to find other languages easier to learn and many become excellent linguists. They are determined that Icelandic should not be corrupted and and a special academic committee has been formed to find Icelandic words for international terms such as 'computer' and 'mobile phone'.

Iceland has always produced accomplished writers and poets (*skalds*), from the writers of the Sagas and Eddic poems to the present day. In the 19th century, **Jónas Hallgrímsson** was a well-loved romantic poet who was at the forefront of the independence movement and the first Icelander to have a statue raised in his memory. The most

▼ *Below: A wedding in Akureyri. Many Icelanders, however, will live together rather than marry.*

important literary figure of the 20th century was undoubtedly **Hálldór Kiljan Laxness**, the winner of the 1955 Nobel Prize for Literature. A one-time monk, communist and film writer, he spent much of his life living abroad, but his novels were largely about the harsh conditions of rural life in Iceland.

Not surprisingly, interest in **books** in Iceland is great. There are over 35 publishers in the country printing over 1500 new titles annually. This is the highest book per capita ratio in the world. There are numerous bookshops, particularly in Reykjavík. In addition, there are five national daily **newspapers**, plus regional papers and countless special-interest magazines. Furthermore there are four TV channels, a national theatre and opera house, many art galleries and numerous museums – not bad for a population of just over 300,000!

Religion

The established church in Iceland is the **Evangelical Lutheran Church**, which was made the national church after the Reformation in 1550. Some 96% of the population claim to be Protestants, although only a small fraction attend churches on a regular basis. There are a small number of Roman Catholics, Jehovah's Witnesses and pagan followers of Thor.

Icelanders' attitude towards **marriage** has never been particularly serious. In fact, around 70% of first-born children are born to unmarried parents. Single mothers are not frowned upon (a recent president of the country was a single parent), and children are welcomed, whatever the circumstances of their birth.

The Role of Women

Women were given the right to vote in national elections in 1915. They marked the start of the United Nations Women's Decade in 1975 by holding a one-day strike, bringing the whole of Iceland to a standstill. As well as Iceland having a female president, a Women's Alliance political party was also formed and soon gained representation in parliament. This frightened the other political parties so much that they put forward a number of female candidates, which has resulted in the Icelandic parliament having some 22% female MPs. On the employment front, almost 90% of women in Iceland are employed outside the home, but their salaries are still little more than half those of men.

▲ *Above: This turf church in Núpsstaður is the smallest church in Iceland.*

ELVES AND TROLLS

A recent survey found that 53% of Icelanders believed in fairies! Well, let us qualify that – 53% of Icelanders were not prepared to deny their existence. In fact, 5% of the population claim to have actually met a fairy, an elf, a troll or one of the 'hidden people'. In a country where the overwhelming majority claim to be Christians, these statistics are perhaps a little surprising. While ghosts were traditionally malevolent beings in Icelandic history, elves tended to be more welcome, and today modern Icelanders are happy to live alongside them – they consider the existence of elves to be a 'pleasant idea'.

INTRODUCING ICELAND

POPULATION

Population: 325,600 (Jan 2014 estimate)
Ages: 0–14 years: 23.18%
15–64 years: 65.01%
65 and over: 11.81%
Population growth rate:
0.38%
Birth rate:
14.62 births/1000 people
Death rate: 6.1/1000 people
Sex ratio: (male:female)
at birth: 1.08
under 15 years: 1.07
15–64 years: 1.02
65 years and over: 0.81
Life expectancy at birth:
male: 80.8 years (2012)
female: 83.9 years (2012)
Infant mortality: 0.9/1000
live births (2011)

CHURCH ARCHITECTURE

The church architecture in Iceland ranges from small turf chapels built by local farmers, often no bigger than a garden shed, to large Lutheran cathedrals on which no expense has been spared. In between are village churches in typical Nordic style with red corrugated iron roofs, simple towers and plain interior fittings. The modern churches with a geological theme are memorable and everyone will want to see the **Hallgrímskirkja** in Reykjavík, with its basalt-like columns. The same architect produced a smaller version in **Akureyri**. Don't miss the church in **Blönduós**, which is designed like a volcano, complete with a crater.

Education

Iceland claims **100% literacy** and certainly education standards are very high. Because of the remoteness of the rural areas of Iceland, many children have to attend boarding school from an early age. Those students who go on to complete the secondary grammar stage will be nearly 20 years of age. There are over 5000 students at the University of Iceland in Rekjavík and at its outpost at Akureyri, and usually around 3000 Icelandic students at foreign universities.

Health

Iceland has an excellent National Health service, which is free to all. Icelanders have one of the greatest **life expectancy** figures in the world. Women can expect to live to 83.9 years, men 80.8 – a record which only the Japanese can better. Public health care is no doubt a contributing reason for this, but an unpolluted environment and a healthy fish-based diet are also important factors.

Arts and Crafts

Iceland has a long tradition of landscape **painting**, particularly since the beginning of the 20th century. Stalwarts include Ásgrímur Jónsson (1876–1959),

Jóhannes Kjarval (1885–1972) and Jón Stefánsson (1881–1962), whose work can be seen in numerous museums and galleries in Reykjavík. Visitors will soon appreciate Iceland's love of **sculpture**, starting at Keflavík airport, the environs of which have some striking modern pieces of work. Statues abound in Reykjavík and other towns, often representing poets and Icelandic heroes rather than politicians and generals. The best-known of the Icelandic sculptors are Ásmundur Sveinsson (1893–1982) and Sigurjón Ólafsson (1908–82), both of whom have museums devoted to their work in Reykjavík.

Icelandic **craft** work consists mainly of pottery and woollen goods. Many visitors take home woollen jumpers in traditional patterns, which are made from the fleece of the Icelandic sheep. The fleeces contain natural oils which keep out water and the soft inner wool makes a good insulation. The most popular line in ceramics is 'lavaware', which has pieces of lava fired into the clay, but discriminating buyers might consider it to be rather garish.

Food and Drink

Eating out is a major expense for the visitor to Iceland, largely because many food items have to be imported. Icelandic food has traditionally been based on **lamb** and **fish**, which are the most commonly available products. In the past they were preserved for the winter in a variety of ways: smoked, pickled, dried and salted, methods which are reflected in the way in which they are served today. Many of the fish, which include cod, her-ring, halibut, haddock, salmon and trout, will be familiar to visitors. Other traditional foods include whale steaks, seal, and even sea birds such as puffins. The lack of fresh **vegetables** means that main courses are usually accompanied by such items as potatoes, pickled cabbage

> ### Friday Night
>
> Iceland appears to foreigners to be a sedate country, so it is something of a surprise for them to find that the nightlife in Reykjavík is amongst the liveliest in Europe. With the high cost of living, youngsters seem to save everything for a huge binge on Friday nights. From 23:00, the whole downtown area of the city is taken over by partying, clubbing young people who move from one venue to the next in what is known as the rúntur. Celebrations go on till three or four in the morning. No point trying to sleep – join them!

◄ *Opposite: Modern sculpture at Keflavík Airport depicting, a bird emerging from its egg.*
▼ *Below: Drying fish at Flateyri, northwest Iceland.*

Early Icelanders needed to conserve food for winter. Not wishing to waste any part of the animal or fish, this led to some unusual food specialities. The sheep, for instance, provides *Súrsaðir hrútspungar*, or pickled rams testicles; *svið*, singed sheep's head complete with eyes; and *slátur*, a collection of sheep's leftovers boiled in a sheep's stomach, much like haggis. The most alien of all to foreigners is *hákari*, or putrefied shark meat. There are, however, more acceptable traditional dishes, such as Christmas meals of *Hanmgikjöt* (smoked lamb) and *rjúpa* (mature ptarmigan cooked in milk gravy). One result of the financial crisis in Iceland and the general tightening of belts has been a resurgence in the popularity of many of these traditional dishes.

▼ *Below: Lounging in hot tubs is a popular activity throughout Iceland.*

and tinned peas or carrots. The growth of the geothermally heated greenhouse industry has served to encourage the appearance of various **salads** on many an Icelandic menu in recent years. **Desserts** are usually in the form of cake or dairy produce.

Restaurants in Iceland are generally rather expensive, particularly those in hotels. Fortunately, some offer 'tourist menus' – usually consisting of soup, main course and coffee – at a fixed price, which is normally slightly lower at lunch time. American-style fast-food restaurants are common and popular in Reykjavík, but scarce in other parts of the country. A cheap option at kiosks and petrol stations is the **hot dog** (*pylsur*), which is enormously popular with Icelanders.

The price of **alcoholic drinks** in Iceland is astronomical and visitors are advised to bring their own supplies into the country. Strong beer was prohibited until 1989. Now strong beers from abroad are on sale, and Icelandic beer is also excellent. Wines can be bought with meals but are extremely expensive. The local spirit is *brennivín*, a type of schnapps made from corn and flavoured with caraway seeds. It is known as 'Black Death' because of the label, which the government decreed should be black in an attempt to reduce consumption.

Sport and Recreation

Iceland's most popular recreation is surely **swimming**. Although not great competitors, Icelanders love the social activity of simply lolling around in hot, geothermally heated water, even when snow is falling around them. **Football** is very popular and the national team has embarrassed some of the world's top countries in matches in recent years. There are a number of Icelandic professionals who play for clubs overseas, particularly in the English premiership. **Golf** has increased greatly in popularity through the years, and there are more than 50 courses which allow visitors to play. The long winters restrict outdoor activities, so indoor sports are widely played, including **badminton** and **handball**, in which the Icelandic team is one of the best in the world. **Chess** is a national pastime and Iceland boasts no fewer than six grand masters, the highest per capita ratio in the world. **Bridge** is also keenly played, particularly since the national team won the world championship in Japan in 1991. There are **skiing** facilities near many towns in Iceland, although the short hours of daylight in winter are a restricting factor. **Horse riding** was once a necessity for the farming community, though nowadays farming is much more mechanized, and horse riding has become a popular pastime with Icelanders and visitors alike. Freshwater **fishing** is available throughout the country and there are several exclusive salmon fishing clubs. A licence for salmon fishing is extremely expensive, while trout fishing is more reasonably priced. Iceland has become one of the prime venues for **outdoor adventure activities**. Among the activities on offer are hiking and trekking, mountain biking, mountaineering and river rafting. Icelanders also have a fascination with cross-country touring on snowmobiles and in super jeeps.

▲ *Above: Upskiing is one of the more unusual types of recreation in Iceland.*

THE GOLFING PHENOMENON

Considering Iceland's inhospitable climate and lack of daylight for much of the year, it is perhaps surprising that golf has become so popular. There are believed to be at least 50 courses in Iceland, ranging from five-hole tracts built by enthusiastic local farmers to 18-hole international standard courses on the outskirts of Reykjavík. The most novel competition is the Arctic Open at Akureyri, which takes place in midsummer, allowing players to tee off at midnight and play through the night.

2
Reykjavík

When **Ingólfur Arnarson**, Iceland's first recognized settler, threw his high seat pillars (*öndvegissúlur*) overboard, they washed ashore at a small peninsula in southwest Iceland. In the Viking tradition, he decided that this would be the place where he would settle. The year was 874. He called the place Reykjavík, which loosely translates as 'smoky bay', on account of the steam rising from the hot springs in the area. Today, 'smokeless bay' would be a more apt description, as Iceland's capital is one of the least polluted cities in the world. Despite this early settlement, Reykjavík was slow to grow. Two factors, however, accelerated the process. Firstly, in the mid-1700s, a businessman named **Skúli Magnusson** set up a number of local industries in an attempt to break the Danish trade barriers. His small factories attracted workers from the surrounding rural area. Secondly, the **Alþing** (the Icelandic parliament) was relocated, moving from Þingvellir to Reykjavík. Nevertheless, at the beginning of the 19th century, there were still only 300 inhabitants in the town. By the end of the century the population had grown to 2000. The steady growth continued and by Independence Day in 1944 the number of inhabitants stood at 45,000. Today that figure has quadrupled and stands at just under 200,000. Over half of Iceland's population now lives in the capital city.

Reykjavík is the world's most northerly capital and despite its small size it has a university, a National Theatre, a symphony orchestra and an opera house, plus all the other features one would expect to find in a capital city. Visitors to Reykjavík will

DON'T MISS

*** The Hallgrímskirkja: a modernistic church with great views from its tower over the city and harbour.
*** Tjörnin: city-centre lake full of wildfowl; City Hall stands in northwest corner.
*** Harpa: magnificent Concert Hall and Conference Centre.
** Öskjuhlíð: a hilltop crowned by the city's water tanks and a revolving restaurant.
** Bernhöftstorfan: a group of old wooden buildings at the western end of Bankastræti.
** Austurvöllur: a pleasant city square, near parliament and the Lutheran Cathedral.

◄ *Opposite: The distinctive Hallgrímskirkja, Reykjavík's most famous landmark.*

CLIMATE

Reykjavík, the capital city, is located in the wettest and windiest part of the country, facing the full force of the prevailing **southwesterly winds**. In the dark winters, the average temperatures fall to just below freezing point. Spring and autumn are cool, but things improve in **summer** with an average temperature in July of 10.6°C (51°F). **Rainfall** is moderate throughout the year, with a total of 799mm (31.5in), peaking in January and October.

▶▶ *Opposite: Eider ducks are among the many wildfowl found on Tjörnin lake.*
▼ *Below: A variety of buildings and architectural styles on the shore of the Tjörnin.*

find that Icelanders are proud of their landscape and, both in the rural areas and in the city, litter, thankfully, is not tolerated. Street crime, too, is minimal and there is probably no safer city in the world than Reykjavík.

THE OLD TOWN

The old town, where most of the important buildings in Reykjavík are to be found, is a compact area which can easily be covered on foot. The most readily recognizable feature is the **Tjörnin**, or pond – a small lake which is a haven for wildfowl. Built partly over the lake is the new Town Hall, or **Rádhús**. Just to the north is the pleasant square known as the **Austurvöllur**, where Ingólfur Arnarson originally had his hayfields. At the side of the square is the **Aþlingshúsið**, or parliament house, and away to the east are the main shopping streets. Few visitors will want to miss seeing the modern church called the **Hallgrímskirkja**. From the top of its tower a panoramic view stretches across the city's rooftops. Another good view can be had from the **Perlan** (the Pearl), a restaurant perched on top of the city's hot-water storage tanks. Add the many museums and art galleries and there is plenty to occupy the visitor for several days.

Around the Tjörnin ★★★

In the heart of the old town is the **Tourist Information Centre (TIC)**, located in the middle of a group of wooden buildings at Aðalstræti 2. A city map is available, along with a host of brochures, videos and maps of Iceland. The helpful staff can arrange accommodation and book tours. Particularly useful to visitors are the English-language publications *Around Iceland, Around Reykjavík, What's on in Reykjavík* and *Iceland Explorer*. Opening hours are Jun–mid-Sep 08:30–19:00 daily, mid-Sep Mon–Fri 09:00–18:00, Sat 09:00–16:00, Sun 09:00–14:00. Tel: 354 590 1550, email: info@visitreykjavik.is website: www.visitreykjavik.is

From the TIC take the short walk to the **Tjörnin**. Warm springs keep this lake ice-free in winter so it is an all-year-round haven for birds. Identification boards help visitors to name the wildfowl, including the handsome eider ducks, which are found throughout Iceland. Arctic terns, which spend the winter in the Antarctic, breed on rafts in the centre of the lake, and whooper swans can usually be seen in the summer. Over 40 species of birds have been recorded at this lake. In the northwestern corner of the Tjörnin is the **Rádhús**, or Town Hall. It is ultra-modern in design and built partially on stilts over the lake.

EIDER DUCKS

One of the first birds the visitor to Iceland will see is the eider duck, which breeds on the **Tjörnin Lake** in the centre of Reykjavík. The drake is handsome, with black, white and green plumage, while the female is a drab brown. They are essentially **marine ducks**, but will breed on lakes and rivers close to the coast. The female lines the nest with down from her own breast. The **down** has been used for centuries for stuffing pillows. The **eggs** are also eaten, and the eider duck has been semi-domesticated in Iceland. After hatching, the eider ducklings gather together in a crèche, often consisting of over 30 birds, looked after by one or two of the females.

REYKJAVÍK

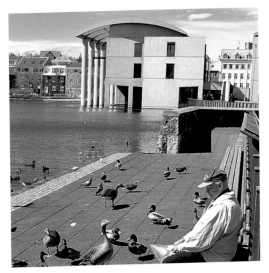

▲ Above: Reykjavík's modern Rádhús, or town hall, is built into the waters of Lake Tjörnin right in the centre of the city.

Completed in 1992, its design was controversial, because many people felt that it was out of place in the old part of the city. The entrance hall is well worth a look – there is an information desk and a huge relief map of Iceland. Away to the southwest of the lake are the modern buildings comprising the **University of Iceland**, which was established in 1911 and now has over 5000 students. Amongst the university buildings is the **Árni Magnússon Institute for Icelandic Studies**, which was named after the man who, in the 18th century, did much to track down the original manuscripts of the Sagas and Eddas. Opening times are Mon–Fri 09:00–12:00 and 13:00–15:00 except public holidays. The Institute is closed for 3–4 weeks each summer (usually mid-Jul–mid-Aug), ask at TIC for details (www.arnastofnun.is). Also on the university site is the **Nordic House**, which acts as a cultural link between Iceland and the other Nordic countries. The Nordic House is open from 09:00–16:30 and has an excellent cafeteria.

Austurvöllur ★★★

Just to the north of the Tjörnin is the attractive square known as the **Austurvöllur**, occupying land which was once Ingólfur Arnarson's farm. In the centre of the square is a **Statue of Jón Sigurðsson** (1811–79), who led the 19th-century independence movement in Iceland. Built on the southern side of the Austurvöllur is the **Alþingishúsið**, or Parliament House. This dull, grey basalt building was constructed in 1881, before Iceland's independence from Denmark, which explains the Danish coat of arms on the front of the building. On the south-

WALKING IN REYKJAVÍK

Many of the sights of compact central Reykjavík can be reached on foot, but the visitor can also access other areas within the city limits by following set **walking trails**. These walks cover the sea shore, heaths and valleys, and usually link up with bus routes. You can expect to be accompanied by joggers and mountain bikers. For further information on Reykjavík's walking trails, contact the **TIC**, tel: 354 590 1550.

eastern side of the Austurvöllur is the **Dómkirkjan**, or Lutheran Cathedral. It dates from 1796, when it was built on the orders of the Danish King. The inside is more interesting than the rather ordinary exterior. Look out for the modern font, made by the Danish sculptor Berthel Thorvaldsen. The Dómkirkjan is open weekdays 10:00–16:30.

Around Arnarhöll ★★★

Located along Lækjargata is the **Stjórnarráðið**, or Government House. Built between 1765 and 1770, this whitewashed building was once a prison, but now contains the offices of the prime minister. A short distance to the north of Government House is a low, grassy hillock known as **Arnarhöll** (Eagle Hill). On the summit is a statue of Ingólfur Arnarson, Iceland's first official settler, shown looking out of his boat towards the land he was to make his home. The most interesting, and oldest, street in the area is **Aðalstræti**, which was where Skúli Magnusson set up his cottage industries in the mid-18th century. The oldest house is number 10, which dates back to 1752. It was once a small weaving workshop, but is now a popular restaurant.

Harpa ★★★

This magnificent Concert Hall and Conference Centre was the work of Danish architects Henning Larsen with interior design

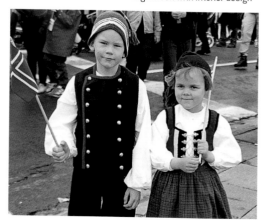

◀ *Left: Icelandic children wear traditional costumes on National Day.*

REYKJAVÍK

CITY OF SCULPTURES

Reykjavík probably has more sculptures per capita than any other major city in the world. The scene is set when the visitor arrives in the country at **Keflavík Airport**, which has a number of huge, eye-catching modern sculptures. Iceland has several important 20th-century sculptors, including **Einar Jónsson, Ásmundur Sveinsson** and **Sigurjón Ólafsson**. Their work, as well as that of contemporary artists, can be found throughout the city. A brochure, describing a **sculpture trail** around the old part of the city, can be obtained from the Tourist Information Centre.

by Olafur Eliasson. With seating for up to 1800, the wonder is that so small a country could afford such a cultural centre. In fact it was due to be larger, with a hotel and luxury apartments, but the economic crash required downsizing. Even so, the completed hall – opened in 2011 – cost over £100million. If you cannot fit in a performance, visit anyway to enjoy the superb interior.

Rooftop Views ★★★

There are two popular places to go for good views over the city: the Hallgrímskirkja and the Öskjuhlíð. **Hallgrímskirkja**, just to the east of the city centre, is often mistaken for the cathedral. Completed in 1974, it was built in memory of the Reverend Hallgrímur Pétursson, a noted composer of hymns. The church has one of the geological designs for which Iceland is noted, with its white-coloured west end built of basalt-like columns, which soar up to a graceful tower, some 75m (246ft) in height. The style of the austere interior is traditional Gothic, but most visitors come to take the lift to the top of the tower accompanied by taped choral music, for the superb view over Reykjavík. The church and tower are open from 09:00–17:00 (www.hallgrims kirkja.is). On the green in front of the Hallgrímskirkja is a statue of Leifur Eiríksson, a gift from the USA to celebrate the 1000th anniversary of the Alþing.

Öskjuhlíð, a hill which overlooks the domestic airport and the bay, is another good viewpoint. The summit has some old bunkers and gun emplacements, relics of World War II. Also perched on top of the hill is a group of hot-water storage tanks which supply the hot water to the city. A revolving restaurant called the **Perlan** (Pearl) is on top of the tanks.

A path from the Öskjuhlíð leads down to the **Nauthólsvik Geothermal Beach**. Golden sand for the beach was imported from Morocco, and that, along with an artificial hot spring and numerous hot tubs, ensures that this is a popular venue for the locals during the summer months.

▼ *Below: The clarity of this panoramic view – from the top of the Hallgrímskirkja tower over Reykjavík – is due to the lack of pollution.*

THE HARBOUR

Reykjavík's harbourside is full of interest. The shoreline here was once marked by **Hafnarstræti** (Harbour Street), but the waterfront was extended during World War II. The Customs House, on Hafnarstræti, has some excellent 19th-century houses on its southern side. The harbourside is the regular venue for the **Kolaportið flea market**, where great bargains

▲ *Above: Of all the artworks in Reykjavík, this harbourside sculpture of a Viking boat, the work of Jón Gunnar Árnason, is the most distinctive.*

can be found, particularly home-made woollen goods. At the western end of the harbour is the **Saga Museum** (Grandagardi 2) with realistic dioramas of important moments in Iceland's history based on information from the Sagas. Open 10:00–18:00 daily, tel: 511 1517, www.sagamuseum.is At the eastern end of the harbour, off Sæbraut, is probably the most remarkable of all the many sculptures in the city; the **Viking Ship**, by Jón Gunnar Árnason, is very photogenic. The harbour is the starting point for boat trips for whale watching and bird observation.

MUSEUMS AND GALLERIES

The National Museum ★★

Founded in 1863, the National Museum moved to its present location on Hringbraut (entrance in Suðurgata) in 1950. It has over 16,000 artefacts from Viking times to the present, including costumes, agricultural implements, nautical equipment, furniture and boats. The most famous item is the wooden church door from Valþjófsstaður. This door was carved in the 13th century and depicts a Norse battle scene. Open May–mid-Sep 10:00–17:00 daily, Oct–April, 13:00–17:00. Suðurgata 41, tel: 530 2200, www.natmus.is

Listasafn Íslands (National Gallery of Iceland) ★

Located just behind the Fríkirkjan (or Free Church) at Fríkirkjuvegur 7, this building has a chequered history. Originally a storage space for ice cut from Lake Tjörnin, it later became a night-

IN PURSUIT OF SALMON

Reykjavík is unique as a capital city in having a first-class salmon river running within its boundaries. But visitors beware! Any salmon caught in Iceland is likely to be one of the most pricey caught anywhere in the world! A licence to catch salmon is extremely **expensive**. Add the price of a guide, equipment and transportation and you have some of the most costly angling imaginable. Fortunately there is the cheaper option of fishing for char and trout. Contact the **Angling Club of Reykjavík**, tel: 568 6050.

▲ *Above: The city's hot water storage tanks are the unusual location for the Pearl Restaurant.*

club, before a fire reduced it to a shell in 1971. It was then reno-vated to house the picture collection from the National Museum. There are also some visiting exhibitions. Open 11:00–17:00 Tue–Sun, tel: 515 9600, www.listasafn.is Admission is free, except for special exhibitions.

Ásmundur Sveinsson Museum ★

Located on Sigtun, in the east of the city, this museum is in a remarkable igloo-shaped building, designed by the sculptor him-self. Although he spent a great part of his life abroad, the themes of Sveinsson's work come from Icelandic folklore. The museum's garden is full of the sculptor's abstract concrete figures. Open daily May–Sep 10:00–17:00, Oct–Apr 13:00–17:00, tel: 553 2155, www.artmuseum.is Ásmundur Sveinsson's house is at Freyjugata 41, opposite the Hallgrímskirkja, and also houses **The Labour Union's Art Gallery**. Open daily 13:00–17:00 except Mon (but closed in Jul), tel: 511 5353.

Einar Jónsson Museum ★

This cube-shaped building, designed by the sculptor, is also near the Hallgrímskirkja. The most mystic of all the Icelandic sculptors, Jónsson's only traditional work is the statue of Jón Sigurðsson in the Austurvöllur Njarðargata. Open Jun–mid-Sep Tue–Sun 13:00–17:00, mid-Sep–May Sat and Sun 13:00–17:00. Closed Dec and Jan, tel: 561 3797, www.lej.is

A MAN-MADE GEYSER

Visitors to the revolving **Pearl Restaurant** on Öskjuhlíð hill are now treated to an additional attraction besides the view. An automatic geyser has been installed. It is not mechanical, but designed on the same principle which causes natural geysers to spout. Superheated geothermal water enters a tapering tube under pressure. Eventually the pressure builds up to such an extent that an eruption of water occurs every five minutes or so. The pipe then refills and the cycle is repeated. The geyser only operates in summer. For exact dates visitors need to check at the TIC or visit www.perlan.is

MUSEUMS AND GALLERIES

Kjarvalsstaðir ★

Located in Miklatún Park, the Kjarvalsstaðir (Municipal Art Gallery) displays the works of Iceland's best-known artist, the surrealist painter Jóhannes Kjarval (1885–1972). His work is displayed in two large rooms, but there are also numerous exhibitions by other painters, both Icelandic and international. Open 10:00–17:00 daily, tel: 517 1290.

Numismatic Museum ★

This museum at Kalkofnsvegur 1, near the Kjarvalsstaðir, houses collections of coins, medals, military decorations and related books. Open Mon–Fri 13:30–15:30, tel: 569 9600.

Natural History Museum ★

Situated at Hverfisgata 116, near Hlemmur bus station, this museum has a large collection of rocks, minerals and indigenous flora and fauna. Open Mon–Thu 10:00–19:00, Fri 11:00–17:00, Sat 13:00–17:00, closed Sun, tel: 570 0430. Admission fee.

Sigurjón Ólafsson Museum ★

This museum, located at Laugarnestangi 70 between Laugardalur and the harbour, displays a collection of this sculptor's work. Open in general daily 14:00–17:00 in summer except Mon, Sat and Sun only 14:00–17:00 in winter, variable with exhibitions, tel: 553 2906. Ask at TIC for details.

Museum of Photography ★

A collection of ancient and modern photographs as well as photographic equipment, at Borgartún 1. Open Mon–Thu 12:00–19:00, Fri 12:00–18:00, weekends 13:00–17:00, tel: 411 6300.

Árbæjarsafn (Open Air Museum) ★

Based on a mid-15th-century farm on the eastern outskirts of the city, Árbæjarsafn is a collection of ancient farm buildings

NORTHERN LIGHTS

Although the main tourist season in Iceland is a short one, many visitors come to the country in winter to see the Northern Lights. The scientific name is *Aurora borealis*, named after the Roman goddess of dawn, Aurora, and the Greek name for the north wind, Boreas. The lights shine above the sky in red and green, largely between latitudes 65 and 72 degrees north of the Equator. They are formed when particles in the solar wind collide with hydrogen, nitrogen and oxygen, the earth's magnetic field trapping the particles. The results can be spectacular, but a clear night is needed, along with an absence of light pollution at ground level.

▼ *Below: The Natural History Museum has some fine geological specimens.*

Swimming is undoubtedly the most common pastime in Iceland. Swimming lessons are compulsory in schools and no student can graduate from secondary school without passing a swimming test. Reykjavík has no fewer than **nine swimming pools**, all open air, thanks to the country's geothermal water, which is a compensation for the cool climate. Icelanders love soaking in a hot pool with snow falling on them! Visitors using the pools should remember that a **high standard of hygiene** is expected. It is compulsory to wash and soap thoroughly (including the hair), without a swimsuit on, before entering a pool. Enjoy the **hot pots** around the pool. These are a type of jacuzzi, with temperatures kept at around 44°C (108°F).

and homes from around the country, and reassembled on the site. They include a turf church (1842) from the Skagafjörður area, numerous barns and a sheep hut. There are also transport items, including the only locomotive to run in Iceland (used to construct Reykjavík harbour). Open Jun–Aug daily 10:00–17:00, Sep–May guided tours only daily at 13:00 or by appointment, tel: 411 6300. Admission fee.

Reykjavík 871 +/-2

This fascinating museum is based around a Viking longhouse dated at around 871, which was discovered when the Hotel Centrum was built. Artefacts recovered show that the inhabitants were farmers, hunters and fishermen, who knew how to smelt metals. Open daily 10:00–17:00. Located at Aðelstræti 16, tel: 411 6370, www.reykjavík871.is

Icelandic Phallological Museum This (tel: 561 6663, www.phallus.is) is surely one of the most bizarre museums anywhere in the world. It contains a collection of over 300 species of penises from a variety of animals. Although there are no human contributions, it is said that a number of men have bequeathed their private parts on their death! Open May–Sep daily 10:00–18:00, Oct–Apr daily 11:00–18:00.

OTHER PLACES OF INTEREST

Höfði House ★

This building in Borgartún, close to the shore, is used for civic receptions and functions. Its main claim to fame is that it was the venue for the Reagan–Gorbachev summit in 1986. There is a superb sculpture in the front of the building by Sigurjón Ólafsson. Not open to the public.

Botanical Gardens ★

Approximately 65% of Iceland's plants are found in the Botanical gardens, located in the Laugardalur area in the east of the city. The collection was started by an enterprising local citizen and bought by the city authorities in 1955. Open May–Sep daily 10:00–22:00, Oct–Apr daily 10:00–15:00.

▲ *Above: Children enjoy a puppet show on the shores of Lake Tjörnin.*

Viðey Island ★ ★ ★

Reached by ferry from Skarfabakki pier, and by tour operators. Important historical site, but now more famous for Yoko Ono's **Imagine Peace Tower**, a memorial to John Lennon. The tower comprises 15 searchlights and prisms which generate a column of light which is claimed to reach 4000m (12,000ft) and is visible for miles.

Laugadalur ★

This open space located in the east of the city is the main sport and recreation area. It has Reykjavík's largest open-air geothermally heated swimming pool, a football stadium, ski slopes, the Botanical Gardens, a zoo and an ice-skating rink. Don't miss the curious Old Wash House (where, in times past, washerwomen scrubbed the city's laundry), and the Family Fun Park and Zoo.

Ellidaár River ★

Reykjavík is probably the only capital city in the world with a salmon fishing river within its boundaries. The Ellidaár River is in the eastern suburbs and is fed from Lake Ellidaár (which is excellent for trout fishing). The best time to watch the salmon leaping their way upstream is during late July and early August.

> **WHERE ARE ALL THE CATS AND DOGS?**
>
> It slowly dawns on visitors that Icelanders keep few pets. Cats are rarely seen and any dogs noticed are likely to be working animals on farms. In fact, the Iceland government decided that it was unhygenic to keep dogs in city apartments and for years they were banned in Reykjavík. The law has recently been repealed, but dogs are still rare in the city.

REYKJAVÍK

▲ *Above: Traditional wooden houses in the inner suburbs of Reykjavík, with the spire of the Hallgrímskirkja in the distance.*

DOMESTIC ARCHITECTURE

Builders in Iceland have always had a shortage of timber. Even driftwood found on the beach was a valuable commodity. Wealthy people could import wood from Norway. Stone was impractical for building as volcanic rock, particularly lava, can rarely be cut to suitable shapes. For the ordinary person turf was the common building material, so it is not surprising that few buildings have survived from before the 18th century. During the 20th century, materials such as concrete and corrugated iron became available and these are dominant today. Most Icelanders live in detached houses, but in Reykjavík there are some low-rise apartment blocks of imaginative design.

ENTERTAINMENT IN REYKJAVÍK

Reykjavík's **National Theatre** is located at Hverfisgata 19. It does perform operas and ballets, but concentrates mainly on plays. The building itself is of interest, with the interior said to be inspired by the basaltic columns of the Svartifoss waterfall in Southern Iceland. Reykjavík also has a **Symphony Orchestra** and an **Opera Company**; the main tourist office will have details of performances; tel: 551 1200, www.leikhusid.is There are several **cinemas** in the city, some of which are multi-screen. Films are screened in their original language and have Icelandic subtitles. There are three **shows** which will appeal to tourists. The **Volcano Show** is based in a small film theatre at Hellusund 6a near Tjörnin Lake; tel: 845 9548. The films are the work of two Icelandic photographers who have recorded all the eruptions in the country for the last 40 years, and include the award-winning *Birth of an Island*, describing the growth of Surtsey in the Westmann Islands. The Volcano Show is essential viewing for all visitors going on to the volcanic parts of the country. There are three performances a day in English, and also programmes in French and German. The **Volcano House** at 11 Tryggvagata (tel: 555 1900), in the Old Town, has a good geological exhibition and also shows two fine films on the 1973 eruption in the Westmann Islands and the 2010 Eyjafjallajökull eruption which stopped European air traffic. Each lasts about 25 minutes and are shown on the hour every hour from 10:00–21:00 daily (even at Christmas and New Year, though for shorter times). The shows are essential viewing for all visitors going on to the volcanic parts of the country. **Light Nights**, which is shown at Baldursgata 37, is performed in English and is an interesting account of the settlement of Iceland and of the Sagas. Contact the TIC for performance times. There are a vast number of **pubs** and **discos** in Reykjavík, but none are cheap. They are crowded at weekends, but rarely start to liven up until around 23:00. Contact the TIC for further details.

GREATER REYKJAVÍK

Stretching away from the city centre are very pleasant suburbs of detached houses and low-rise apartment blocks. As more and more Icelanders move from the rural areas to the capital city, the suburbs of Reykjavík advance across the lava plains. The skill of Iceland's architects ensures that even the apartments have a certain flair and the design is never dull. Gardens are attractive and there are probably more mature trees in Reykjavík than in the rest of the island. Amongst the suburbs is the occasional shopping mall, such as the modern **Kringlan Centre** in the east of the city. Further out is Greater Reykjavík, with its rather characterless settlements. An exception is **Hafnarfjörður**, which is an interesting town in its own right.

Located at the end of the Reykjavík Peninsula is the suburb of **Seltjarnarnes**, from where there are often good views across the sea northwards to the icecap of Snæfellsjökull. The Pharmacy Museum is housed in an 18th-century stone building in Seltjarnarnes. Open Jun–Aug Tue, Thu and weekends 13:00–17:00, tel: 561 7100. Immediately to the south of the city is the suburb of **Kópavogur**. Its main claim to fame is that, with 20,000 residents, it is Iceland's second largest community. Kópavogur's Smáralina Centre is the largest shopping mall in Iceland. Further south is **Garðabær**, which is considered to be Reykjavík's most elite suburb. Away to the southwest is **Hafnarfjörður** which, although part of Greater Reykjavík, is a town in its own right and is therefore described in Chapter 3, which deals with the Reykjanes Peninsula. East of Reykjavík, and immediately outside its boundary, is the fast-growing town of **Mosfellsbær**, with a population approaching 5000.

A very popular excursion from Reykjavík is a trip to **Viðey Island**, located a few kilometres north of the mainland. During summer, ferries run hourly from Sundahöfn harbour to Viðey. The island, which is situated on an extinct volcano, has been a religious centre since the 12th century and the second oldest church in Iceland is found here. There are some pleasant walks, fine basalt cliffs and an up-market restaurant.

▼ *Below: A lift takes visitors to the top of Hallgrímskirkja, from which there are stunning views over the city and the harbour.*

REYKJAVÍK

BEST TIME TO VISIT

Because of the climate and relative hours of daylight and darkness, most tourists visit during the **summer** peak season of June–August. Tourist authorities want to extend the season into spring and autumn with 'city breaks' to Reykjavík, where the lively nightlife attracts visitors at times such as New Year.

GETTING THERE

The majority of visitors arrive by plane via Keflavík Airport, some 48km (30 miles) from Reykjavík. Buses meet every incoming flight, departing 45 minutes after arrival and taking travellers to the coach station. Some buses from the airport also stop at hotels in Reykjavík and nearby areas, see www.re.is/flybus for details. Both the Blue Lagoon and the Keflavík and Icelandair hotels in Keflavík offer transport to/from the airport. Visitors using the car ferry will arrive at Seydisfjörduron on the east coast and have a long car or coach journey of around 740km (460 miles) to Reykjavík using the Ring Road.

GETTING AROUND

Reykjavík's **taxis** are cheaper than one might expect and tipping is not required. **Bicycles** can be hired economically, but the frequent wind in Reykjavík makes cycling difficult. **Buses** offer cheap and convenient transport and the two main terminals are at Lækjartorg and Hlemmur (which has a tourist information desk). A free map of the bus routes is provided by the TIC. There is a standard fare for all routes and distances. Drivers do not give change. The **Reykjavík Tourist Card** (obtained from the City Hall) provides unlimited use of the city's buses and free admission to some museums and swimming pools. Kids will enjoy the hop-on hop-off bus which connects all the major places of interest and has recorded commentaries in six languages.

WHERE TO STAY

A range of luxury international **hotels**, **guesthouses** and **hostels**. A significant number close during winter. **Camp sites** only open in summer.

Luxury

101 Hótel, Hverifisgata 10, 101, tel: 580 0101, www.101hotel.is Contemporary boutique hotel; popular restaurant/bar, spa and art gallery.

Hótel Borg, Pósthússtræti 11, 101, tel: 551 1440, fax: 551 1420, www.hotelborg.is Art Deco hotel located on Austurvöllur Square.

Hótel Reykjavík Centrum, Aðalstræti 16, 101, tel: 514 6000, www.hotelcentrum.is Spreads over three ancient buildings.

Grand Hótel Reykjavík, Sigtún 38, 105, tel: 514 8000, www.grand.is Business hotel; quiet location near Kringlan Centre.

Mid-range

Guesthouse Aurora, Freyjugata 24, 101, tel: 899 1773, e-mail: book@aurorahouse.is website: www.aurorahouse.is Attractive traditional house.

Anna Guesthouse, Smáragötu 16, 101, tel: 562 1618, www.guesthouseanna.is Beautifully decorated guesthouse; in former Czechoslovakian embassy.

Hótel Alda, Langavegur 66, tel: 553 9366, www.aldahotel.is New hotel in the heart of the old city.

Budget

Guesthouse Baldursbrá, Laufásvegur 41, 101, tel: 552 6646, fax: 562 6647, http://notendur.centrum.is/~heijfis Simple, basic rooms, shared bathrooms and hot tub. Generous buffet breakfast.

HI Youth Hostel, Sundlaugavegur 34, 105, tel: 553 8110, fax: 588 9201. Next to camp site in Laugardalur. Closed 20 Dec–5 Jan. Booking essential in summer.

Salvation Army Guesthouse, Kirkjustræti 2, 101, tel: 561 3203, fax: 561 3315, www.guesthouse.is Simple rooms in the heart of the city.

Camping

The camp site at **Laugardalur** is open 15 May–15 Sep. It can be crowded in Jul and Aug. Showers, laundry and cooking facilities. Daily morning Flybus to Keflavík Airport.

WHERE TO EAT

There is a range of restaurants in central Reykjavík and the suburbs. Though food is a big expense for visitors, bargains can be found, particularly with lunchtime tourist menus.

Luxury

Perlan (The Pearl), Öskjuhlíð hill, tel: 562 0200, www.perlan. is Spectacularly sited on top of city's water tanks; revolves to give views over Reykjavík.

Lækjarbrekka, Bankastræti 2, tel: 551 4430, www.laekjar brekka.is Gourmet seafood and lamb, traditional building.

Fiskélagið (Fish Company), Vesturgötu 2a, tel: 552 5300. Exquisite food and excellent service, but not cheap.

Mid-range

Café Loki, Lokastigur 28, 101 Reykjavík, tel: 466 2828. Icelandic dishes, including great meat soup and the chance to try a little well-rotted shark.

Asia, Laugavegur 10, tel: 562 6210. Good range of Asian dishes. Take aways also available.

Sólon, Bankastræti 7a, tel: 562 3232. Where the locals eat. Very friendly and wide choice.

Naust, Vesturgata 6–8, tel: 551 7759. Offers a range of seafood.

Budget

Fast-food outlets include **Pizza Hut** (Smáralinn, tel: 533 2000), **Metró** (Austurstræti and Suðurlandsbraut), **Kentucky Fried Chicken** (Faxafen 2, tel: 568 0636) **Kaffi**, Austurstræti, Reykjavík, tel: 552 2615. Good value, hearty meals.

SHOPPING

Reykjavík's main downtown shopping streets are Bankastræti, Laugavegur and Austurstræti. Skólavoðustígur, which connects Laugavegur

with the Hallgrímskirkja, has chic boutiques and craft shops. Many larger shops have moved from the city centre to the **Kringlan Mall**, which has over 100 shops, plus cinemas, pubs, restaurants and banks, making it an 'alternative city centre'. There is also the massive **Smáralind Mall** in Kópavogur. Despite its reputation as an expensive city, you can find bargains in **woollen goods** at the Hand-knitting Association of Iceland (Skólavöðustígur 19, tel: 552 1890). Home-made woollen goods can be bought cheaply at the Kolaportið Flea Market near the harbour. For various crafts, visit Crafts and Design (Aðalstræti 10, tel: 551 7595). Last-minute shopping at Keflavík Airport's duty-free includes Icelandic products such as vacuum-packed fish.

TOURS AND EXCURSIONS

A popular excursion is a relaxing trip to the **Blue Lagoon** in the Reykjanes Peninsula, usually combined with a visit to the Hafnir aquarium or local bird cliffs. Airport transfers also stop here. More demanding is the **Golden Circle Tour**, stopping at the greenhouse town of Hverageroi, the volcanic crater of Keriö, Skálholt Cathedral, Gullfoss, Geysir and Þingvellir. Most travel agencies also offer a **City Tour of Reykjavík**.

The **Icelandic Travel Market**, Bankastræti 2, tel: 562 3045, is a useful starting point for trips out of the city as it has information on companies offering a range of excursions, as well having some tourist information and city maps etc. **Elding Adventures at Sea**, Ægisgaröur 5, tel: 519 5000, www.elding.is offers whale watching (including winter trips) and visits to the Imagine Peace Tower.

USEFUL CONTACTS

Tourist Information Centre, Aðalstræti 2, tel: 590 1550, www.visitreykjavik.is
What's On, Laugavegur 4, tel: 551, 3600, www.whatson.is has information on events in the city and also publishes a regular guide which has details on a month by month basis of concerts etc.

Reykjavík Excursions, Vatns- mýrarvegur 10, tel: 580 5400, www.re.is Operated by BSÍ, the main bus operator runs bus tours to all the local tourist highspots, and also more far-flung tours, e.g. to see the Northern Lights, and glacier snowmobiling.

Farm Holidays, Siðumúll 2, tel: 570 2700, www.farmholidays.is
Guðmundur Jónasson Travel, Borgartún 34, tel: 511 1515, www.gjtravel.is offers coach tours, as well as horse riding, cycle tours, walking tours, adventure travel etc.

REYKJAVÍK	J	F	M	A	M	J	J	A	S	O	N	D
AVE. TEMP.°C	-0.4	-1.6	-1.5	0.4	7.2	9.8	11.6	11.1	6.6	5.0	3.7	-0.3
AVE. TEMP.°F	30.9	29.9	30.4	37.7	44.9	49.6	52.8	51.9	43.8	41.0	38.6	31.4
AVE. RAINFALL mm	75.6	71.8	81.8	58.3	43.8	50	51.8	61.8	66.5	85.6	72.5	78.7
AVE. RAINFALL in	2.97	2.83	3.22	2.29	1.73	1.97	2.04	2.43	2.62	3.37	2.86	3.1

3
Around Reykjavík

The area to the east and south of Reykjavík is the only part of Iceland which some short-term visitors see. Fortunately it boasts many of the essential historical and geological features which make the country so fascinating. The **Mid-Atlantic Ridge** runs through the area from northeast to southwest. Frequent volcanic eruptions over recent geological time have left extensive lava flows on the Reykjanes Peninsula – a desolate scene for travellers arriving at Keflavík Airport. Further inland, there are volcanoes such as **Hekla** and explosion craters such as **Kerið**, but the star attractions are the geothermal features in the **Geysir** region – where the geyser **Strokkur** performs reliably every three minutes or so – along with the amazing **Gullfoss** waterfall.

The area to the east of Reykjavík is one of the most fertile in Iceland and the two main market towns are **Selfoss** and **Hveragerði**. At the latter, the local geothermal heat is harnessed for electricity, which is the basis for a significant greenhouse agriculture, while the lovely lakeside resort of **Laugarvatn** is popular with weekenders from Reykjavík.

This part of Iceland is steeped in history. Most tours visit the religious centre of **Skálholt**, with its small modern cathedral. Away to the northwest is Iceland's largest lake – **Þingvallavatn**. At its northern end is the **Þingvellir** historical area, which was the site of the annual Alþing, an outdoor parliamentary assembly, which first functioned in 930 and witnessed the birth of the modern Icelandic Republic in 1944.

DON'T MISS

*** **Gullfoss:** Iceland's most visited waterfall.
*** **The Great Geysir Area:** fumeroles, mud springs, hot springs and Strokkur geyser.
*** **Þingvellir Historical Site:** location of Iceland's ancient outdoor parliament.
*** **The Blue Lagoon:** bathe in the healthy, warm lake, surrounded by lava flows.
* **Krýsuvíkurberg and Hafnaberg:** sea-bird cliffs on the Reykjanes Peninsula.
* **Kerið:** explosion crater near Selfoss, with the volcano Hekla in the background.

◄ *Opposite: The geyser Strokkur erupts regularly every three to five minutes.*

AROUND REYKJAVÍK

Most historic sites are usually visited in the whirlwind day trip known as the **Grand Circle Tour**. It gives a good insight into the scenery and history of Iceland, but it can be rather exhausting and the sites crammed with tourists and coaches. It is far better to take two days and travel independently out of season. Tourist coaches are less obvious in the Reykjanes Peninsula, except at the **Blue Lagoon**, where the waters are known to cure a variety of skin diseases.

▲ *Above: Four-wheel-drive coaches take tourists on the popular Grand Circle Tour from Reykjavík.*
▶▶ *Opposite: A 'sea-bird city' on the basalt cliffs of Krýsuvíkurberg, located on the southern part of the Reykjanes Peninsula.*

THE REYKJANES PENINSULA

The low peninsula of Reykjanes, just to the south of Reykjavík, juts out into the Atlantic Ocean, facing the full force of the prevailing southwesterly winds. Sitting right on the Mid-Atlantic Ridge, the peninsula is composed largely of lava fields, which are covered with Iceland's ubiquitous grey-green moss. Because of the porous nature of the lava, there are no surface streams and only one lake of any substantial size.

Around Reykjavík

Hafnarfjörður *

Known as the 'gateway to the Reykjanes Peninsula', Hafnarfjörður, with its population of some 25,000 people, has lately been swallowed up by Greater Reykjavík. However, it is a town in its own right in an administrative sense, having a long history as a trading port, with English merchants controlling the town in the early 15th century, until they were thrown out by the Germans. They, in turn, succumbed to the Danish Trade Monopoly in 1602. The port and fishing industries are still thriving and the town has developed a reputation as a cultural centre. There are a number of museums in Hafnarfjörður, the best being the **Hafnarfjörður Folk Museum**, situated at Vesturgata 8. It is housed in a 19th-century warehouse appropriately close to the harbour. Open Jun–Aug 11:00–17:00 daily, other months weekends only 11:00–17:00, tel: 585 5500. The **Institute of Culture and Fine Art** at Strandgata 34 stages concerts and exhibitions. It has a pleasant coffee shop with fine harbour views. Open daily 12:00–17:00 (21:00 Thu) but closed Tue. The highlight in Hafnarfjörður is the annual **Viking Festival** held on the longest day of the year in June. It attracts visitors from all over the world and features strong man competitions, combat exhibitions, folk dancing, longboat trips and traditional Viking foods.

Located immediately to the north of Hafnarfjörður, at the end of the Álftanes Peninsula, is the historic estate of **Bessastaðahreppur**, which is now the official residence of the Icelandic head of state.

In the centre of the Álftanes Peninsula is the skiing area of **Bláfjöll** (Blue Mountains). The hills here rise to 702m (2300ft). There are a number of downhill runs and cross-country ski trails, together with chair and rope lifts.

Reykjanesfólkvangur *

South of Hafnarfjörður, situated in the centre of the peninsula, is the national nature reserve of Reykjanesfólkvangur which covers some 775km² (300 sq miles). In amongst the hiking tracks are some amazing lava formations and, in the south of the reserve, a geothermal area known as Krýsuvík with impressive mud springs, solfataras and steaming vents. In the middle of the reserve is **Lake Kleifavatn**. Its blue waters cover some 10km² (6 sq miles) and it is reputed to be nearly 100m (328ft) deep. Inevitably there are tales of a resident monster. A recent earthquake partially drained the lake and where the water went, nobody knows. Trout fishing is possible here. At the extreme south of the reserve are the sea-bird cliffs of **Krýsuvíkurberg**. Look for three species of guillemot, kittiwakes, razorbills and, at the top of the cliffs, puffins. The island of **Eldey**, 14km (9 miles) offshore, is reputed to be the place where the last great auk was killed. Today Eldey has one of the world's largest gannet colonies.

▶▶ *Opposite: One of several modern sculptures at Leifur Eiríksson International Airport. Made of aluminium and coloured glass, it represents a rainbow.*
▶ *Right: Visitors stroll towards the fumeroles, hot springs and geysers of the Krýsuvík geothermal area.*

The Western Towns ★

The town of Keflavík is a long-established trading port and still has one of the largest fishing fleets in Iceland. It has merged with the neighbouring village of **Njarðvík** to form a settlement of around 10,000 people. Keflavík is best known for being the site of the US-operated NATO military base. American troops came here in 1941 during World War II, replacing British soldiers, with the aim of preventing a German occupation of Iceland. They finally pulled out in September 2006. Keflavík is also the site of the **Leifur Eiríksson International Air Terminal**. The ultra-modern building was built with US help and opened in 1987. The airport grounds are noted for their large modern sculptures, which were the result of a competition. Particularly impressive are sculptures of a rainbow and a bird breaking out of an egg.

In the 'toe' of the peninsula are the two somewhat unremarkable fishing villages of **Garður** and **Sandgerði**. Here, some fish processing takes place. Further south is the deserted village of **Bátsendar**, destroyed by a freak wave in 1798. More picturesque is the fishing village of **Hafnir**, midway down the west coast. It has a fine 19th-century wooden church and some restored houses. A 10-minute walk along the cliffs southwards leads to the sea-bird cliffs of **Hafnaberg**.

The only settlement of any size on the south coast of the peninsula is the fishing port of **Grindavík**, which has around 2300 inhabitants. The port has a long trading history and was used by English and German merchants in the late middle ages. One astonishing historical fact is that it was raided

THE NATO BASE

Some 5000 US servicemen were stationed at the Keflavík NATO base, arousing strong opinions among Icelanders. The country has no armed services of its own. Many saw the US troops as an occupying army, particularly since the thawing of the Cold War. But the base provided considerable employment. Over 900 Icelanders worked at Keflavík and many more gained an indirect living from the US troops. The base closed in 2006, with the perhaps unsurprising result that the town of Keflavík has the highest unemployment rate in Iceland.

in 1627 by Algerian pirates, who took away a large number of the local people as slaves. Fish processing and exporting take place here today. Look out for the moving fishermen's monument, called *Hope*, that shows a fisherman's family looking hopefully out to sea.

▲ *Above: Bathing in the medicinal waters of the Blue Lagoon.*
▶▶ *Opposite: Tomatoes for sale at the roadside. They are grown in geothermally heated greenhouses.*

The Blue Lagoon (Bláa Lónið) ★★★

Midway between Grindavík and Keflavík amongst the black lava fields is the popular tourist venue known as the Blue Lagoon. The pale blue waters of the lagoon are in fact the effluent from the Svartsengi power station. Sea water is heated and then filtered as it passes through the lava. The run-off water, which is rich in minerals, has a temperature of 70°C (158°F), but bathing is restricted to one area of the lagoon where temperatures are a more bearable 40°C (104°F). Algae thrive in the hot water, but die as the water cools, adding to the white silica mud on the lake bottom. It sounds unpleasant, but the lagoon water has been shown to relieve the effects of psoriasis, eczema and other skin ailments. There are basic changing rooms, a restaurant and a guesthouse, plus a luxurious touch – swimmers can be served cocktails on floating tables! With steam rising all around and the space-age power equipment and lava fields in the background, a 'swim' in the lagoon can be one of the great tourist experiences of Iceland. The Flybus airport service to and from Reykjavík stops at the Blue Lagoon; tel: 420 8800, website: www.bluelagoon.com

HEALTH TREATMENT AT THE BLUE LAGOON

The silvery-blue opaque waters of the Blue Lagoon and the white silica mud on its bed have been proven to have great health properties. The cocktail of **minerals** in the water, which comes from up to 1830m (6000ft) below the ground, has eased skin conditions such as psoriasis and eczema. A range of products has been developed, including mineral bath salts, lagoon mud for the face and body, moisturizing cream, and shampoo. Not surprisingly, a complex of facilities opened in 1999 to cope with the 200,000 annual visitors.

Þorlákshöfn ★

In the southeastern corner of the Reykjanes Peninsula, the **ferry port** of Þorlákshöfn is located, where regular ferries leave for the **Westman Islands**. This is the only suitable port in the area between Grindavík and Höfn, which accounts for the long, and often rough, voyage. The ferry boat *Herjólfur* makes a daily return trip to the Westman Islands, weather permitting. The port is named after Saint Þorlákur, who was a bishop of Skálholt during the 12th century and, incidentally, the only Icelander ever to have been canonized by the Roman Catholic Church.

EAST OF REYKJAVÍK

The Ring Road (or Route 1) leaves Reykjavík eastwards, running through lava fields and over a mountain pass, before dropping down to the fertile lowland which is one of the country's richest agricultural areas. The first town of any size is **Hveragerði**, with around 1700 inhabitants, many of whom commute daily to the capital. Hveragerði is located on an active geothermal area and several hot springs and steaming vents are readily seen. The geothermal power has been used to heat numerous greenhouses in which crops such as tomatoes, lettuces, cucumbers and flowers are grown. Bananas and other tropical fruits are also produced, but not in a commercial way – just to prove that it can be done! Not surprisingly, Hveragerði is the site of Iceland's National College of Horticulture. There is a small geyser known as Gryta (or Ogress), which erupts several times daily.

On the outskirts of the town is a health clinic, with mineral and mud baths, physiotherapy and a health-food shop. Coach tours stop at a tourist trap by the name of **Eden**, based on an old geothermal greenhouse and selling locally grown potted plants, fruits, souvenirs, woollen goods and postcards. The next town along the Ring Road is **Selfoss**, a pleasant market town on the banks of the Ólfusá River. Although it has little historical interest, Selfoss makes a good centre for exploring the area to the north.

AROUND REYKJAVÍK

Just to the northwest is a hill called **Ingólfsfjall** which rises to a height of 551m (1808ft). The mound on the top is claimed to be the burial site of Ingólfur Arnarson, but the summit is solid rock, so this is a doubtful assertion.

From Selfoss, Route 35 leads inland to some of Iceland's most popular tourist locations. After a short distance, on the right-hand side of the road, is the explosion crater of **Kerið**. Some 55m (180ft) deep and enclosing a rather menacing green lake, it was one of a crater swarm formed around 3000 years ago. From here there are distant views of the volcano **Hekla**, its summit usually swathed with cloud. Hekla has erupted at least 20 times since the settlement of Iceland, most recently in 1991.

Skálholt ★★

The route then leads to the **religious centre** of Skálholt, marked today by a simple, modern church. Its history goes back to the 11th century, when Gissur the White established the first wooden church here. His son, Ísleifur Gissurason, after an education in Germany, became the **first bishop** of Iceland. Skálholt became an important educational centre and an elaborate wooden cathedral replaced the original church. Dark deeds were to come in the 16th century, when the country converted from Catholicism to the Danish Lutheran religion. Bishop **Jón Arason** (who opposed the reformation) and his two sons were beheaded at Skálholt without trial. Today, there is a memorial to Arason on the road leading to the church. The site was destroyed during an earthquake in 1784 and shortly afterwards the bishopric was moved to Reykjavík. The present memorial church on the site was built in the 1950s. When the foundations were

▼ *Below: Turf buildings were largely a response to the lack of timber available.*

laid, the remains of the original cathedral were discovered, showing that it was twice the size of the new building. The simple church is worth a visit and is distinguished by some excellent modern stained glass as well as a superb altar mosaic by Nina Tryggvadóttir.

Great Geysir ★★★

From Skálholt, the road leads northeast to the Great Geysir area of **Haukadalur**. Plumes of steam and the sulphurous smell can be noted from some distance away. The Great Geysir is prob-

▲ *Above: Unusual religious sculptures carved in stone outside Skálholt's cathedral.*

ably the most famous geyser in the world and gave its name to all phenomena of this type. Geysers are spouting hot springs, and the Icelandic word means 'gusher'. The Geysir area covers around 3km² (1.2 sq miles) and consists of geysers, hot springs, mud springs and fumeroles. All have been given Icelandic names. Unfortunately, Great Geysir no longer erupts (although eruptions can be induced by throwing soap powder into the crater!), but luckily its neighbour **Strokkur** ('a churn') is very active, erupting every three to five minutes to a height of around 20m (66ft). The silica crater of Geysir can be inspected, and also some superb blue hot springs nearby. Redeposited silica and travertine surround the spring, and when this material weathers, a wealth of plants and orchids appear. The Great Geysir area has belonged to a number of landowners, including several Englishmen, one of whom used to charge for admission. In 1935, the land was bought by an Icelandic doctor who then gave it to the nation. There is a convenient hotel nearby, plus a petrol station, cafeteria and camping facilities. At the side of the cafe is the Geysirtofa, an audiovisual exhibition explaining the workings of volcanoes and geysers. The high-

GEOTHERMAL TERMINOLOGY

Geothermal activity is found in areas of active vulcanicity. The main features are:
Geysers: an explosive spout of hot water.
Fumeroles: superheated water turns to steam when the pressure drops as it emerges from the ground.
Solfataras: sulphurous gases escape at the surface, giving the typical 'rotten eggs' smell.
Hot springs: water is heated underground and emerges at the surface.
Mud springs: Hot water mixes with volcanic material and bubbles at the surface.

Geysers are the most spectacular features of geothermal areas. They occur when water is **trapped underground** in a cavern or bowl which is connected to the surface by a pipe. Heat from the surrounding rocks superheats the water trapped in the bowl until the **pressure** is such that water and steam 'explode' and, preceded by a rumbling sound, spew out onto the surface in a spout of hot water. Within seconds, the water subsides back down the pipe and the process starts again.

light is a platform on which you can stand to experience an earthquake measuring 5.1 on the Richter Scale.

Gullfoss ★★★

Route 35 continues briefly until Iceland's most famous **waterfall**, Gullfoss, is reached. The name means 'golden falls', after the persistent rainbows which are formed by the spray on sunny days. The **River Hvítá**, swollen by melting snow and ice in the interior, drops some 32m (105ft) over two falls. Above and below Gullfoss is a 2.5km (1.5-mile) gorge up to 70m (230ft) deep.

Last century the falls were under threat of hydroelectric development and a local farmer's wife, Sigrídur Tómasdóttir,

▲ Above: The geyser Strokkur begins to erupt. Every three to five minutes, clouds of steam and water burst up to 20m (65ft) in height.
▶ Right: Gullfoss is Iceland's best-known waterfall. The name means 'golden falls', named after the rainbow formed by the sun and spray.

walked all the way to Reykjavík to protest against this, threatening to throw herself down the falls if the plan went ahead. A memorial to Sigríður stands high above the falls. A footpath from the car park leads down to a viewing platform between the two falls – be sure to take waterproofs as the spray is penetrating.

Laugarvatn *

Southwest of Geysir and Gullfoss is the **spa resort** of Laugarvatn, situated on the shores of a lake of the same name. The name means 'warm lake', and a hot spring nearby called **Vígdalaug** was the traditional place for Christian baptisms by the early bishops of Skálholt. Today, Laugarvatn is an **educational centre**, with a number of colleges which convert to hotels during the summer. The area is a very popular weekend retreat for the inhabitants of Reykjavík, who come for camping, sailboarding and the steam baths.

Þingvellir ***

The Golden Circle Tour's last stop is at Þingvellir, the site of the ancient outdoor parliament, or Alþing. The setting is very dramatic, being at the northern end of Þingvallavatn, Iceland's largest lake. It is also right on the Mid-Atlantic Ridge, where the European and North American plates are moving apart. The site is bordered by parallel fissures, namely **Hrafnagjá** in the east and **Almannagjá** in the west. In the early days, the Öxará river was diverted along the Almannagjá to form some rather impressive falls. Just above the bridge over the Öxará is a 'drowning pool' where adulteresses and witches were thrown (delinquent men were usually decapitated). There are numerous historical sites here. The **Lögberg** or 'law rock' on the western side of the river was where the law-speaker was obliged annually to recite the laws of

▼ Below: Þingvellir is situated on the edge of the 5km-wide fault that divides the American Plate from the European Plate.

AROUND REYKJAVÍK

▶ *Right: Þingvellir Historical Site, where the 39 chieftains would meet annually to review the laws of the country.*

the land from memory. The spot is marked today by a flagpole and plaque. Just east of the Lögberg, on lower ground, was the **Lögretta**, which was the meeting place of the Law Council of 39 chieftains who would discuss new laws. Scattered around the site are the remains of stone *búdir* or **booths** set up by each chieftain for the two-week duration of the Alþing. They were used for shelter and as business premises. There are a number of buildings on the site. The **Church** was built in 1859 and is the last of many to have occupied the Alþing area. It has a number of relics from past buildings. The cemetery, or **Skáldareitur**, just behind the church, is usually referred to as the 'Poets' Graveyard', although no contemporary poets seem to have selected this as their last resting place. The long **farmhouse** nearby is used as a summer home for the prime minister of Iceland and also contains the offices of the National Park Warden. There are a number of water-filled chasms in the area and one of these, the **Peningagjá**, has developed into a wishing well. The unobtrusive wooden **Hótel Valhöll** on the eastern side of the river occupied the site of Snorri Sturluson's old booth. Sadly, the hotel burnt down in July 2009 and in the present economic climate there is unlikely to be any haste to rebuild it. The region around Þingvellir is excellent hiking country, with a number of well-marked trails. It is also possible to drive around the lake on the narrow gravel roads, but traffic can get busy during the summer months.

Þingvellir Historical Site

BEST TIME TO VISIT

The Blue Lagoon is popular all year, and the rest of the area is a **summer** destination from May–Sep. Be prepared for crowds at major sites, particularly Gullfoss, Geysir and Þingvellir in Jul and Aug.

GETTING AROUND

Tour coaches and BSÍ buses connect the major sites from Jun to Sep, but can be infrequent. The BSÍ (tel: 562 1011, www.bsi.is) Omnibus Pass is available at the BSÍ bus terminal in Reykjavík or at airline offices and travel agents. Strætó (tel: 540 2700, www.straeto.is) offers services to some destinations east of Reykjavík.

WHERE TO STAY
Reykjanes Peninsula
Luxury
Hótel Keflavík, Vatnsnesvegi 12, 230 Keflavík, tel: 420 7000, fax: 420 7002, www.hotelkeflavik.is Everything for the air traveller; jacuzzi, sauna, elegant dining.

Mid-range
Northern Light Inn, Blue Lagoon, tel: 426 8650, www.nli.is Bungalow type hotel, walking distance to the Blue Lagoon, and free shuttle to the airport.

Budget
Start Hostel, 637 Lindarbraut, Keflavík, tel: 420 6050. Recently renovated. No airport shuttle but only 8 minutes by taxi.
Camp site Grindavík, tel: 660 7323/420 1100. New state of the art site.

East of Reykjavík
Luxury
Hótel Ranga, 851 Hella, South Iceland, tel: 487 5700, www.hotelranga.is Countryside resort in rustic log cabin style. Gourmet restaurant; many facilities.
Hótel Örk, Breidumork 1c, 810 Hveragerði, tel: 483 4700, www.hotelork.is Health resort; pool and sauna, nine-hole golf course and other outdoor activities. Gourmet restaurant using locally grown organic ingredients.

Mid-range
Hótel Gullfoss, Brattholt, 801 Selfoss, tel: 486 8979, www.hotelgullfoss.com Excellent new hotel near the waterfall.
Hótel Geysir, Haukadal, 801 Selfoss, tel: 480 6800, www.geysircenter.is Geothermal pool and hotspots, restaurant.

Budget
Lambastadir Guesthouse, Lambastadir, 801 Selfoss, tel: 777 0705. Comfortable; geothermal tub. 7 miles east of Selfoss on Highway 1.
Selfoss Hostel, Austurvegur 28, tel: 660 6999/482 1600. Hot tub and hammock.

Camping
Camp sites at Geysir, Laugarvatn, Hveragerði, Reykholt, Þingvellir.

WHERE TO EAT
The best (but most expensive) restaurants are in hotels. The restaurants at Keflavík Hotel and Flughótel in Keflavík offer good menus.

Reykjanes Peninsula
Mid-range
Jenny by the Blue Lagoon, tel: 426 8283. Restaurant and bistro overlooking the lagoon.
Olsen Olsen, Hafnargata 17, Keflavík, tel: 421 4457. American 50s-style theme.

Budget
Restaurant Vör, Grindavík, tel: 426 8570. Overlooks the harbour.

East of Reykjavík
Mid-range
Lindin, Laugarvatn, tel:486 1262. Restaurant and pizzeria overlooking the lake. Local ingredients used, including reindeer and sea birds.

Budget
There are good **snack bars** attached to petrol stations at Selfoss and Geysir.

USEFUL CONTACTS
Regional Tourist Information Centres: Leifur Eiríksson Airport, in the arrivals hall, tel: 570 7799; Selfoss at Eyrvegur 2, tel: 899 8663; Selfoss at Hótel Selfoss, tel: 480 2500; Hveragerði, tel: 483 4601.
Þingvellir National Park Information Service Centre, tel: 482 2660. Best information on weather and road conditions is www.vegagerdin.is/english The **ferry to the Westman Islands** (the *Herjólfur*), which departs from Landeyjahöfn, is run by Eimskip, tel: 481 2800, www.eimskip.is

4
West and Northwest Iceland

This chapter covers the region immediately to the north of Reykjavík as far as the Northwest Fiords. This is a region of wide contrasts, both physically and socially. In the south of the area are the two scenically attractive fiords of **Hvalfjörður**, once the centre of Iceland's whaling operations, and **Borgarfjörður**, which is associated with the *Egils Saga*, and the main towns of **Akranes** and **Borgarnes**, site of the new **Settlement Centre**. Inland, the village of **Reykholt** has strong links with the 13th-century statesman and writer **Snorri Sturluson**.

The **Snæfellsnes Peninsula** juts out into the ocean and has a number of small fishing settlements scattered around its coastline. At the western end is the icecap of **Snæfellsjökull**, which, on a clear day, can be seen all the way from Reykjavík, 100km (60 miles) away.

The **Northwest Fiords** area is one of the remotest parts of the country. Here, most forms of communication between the small, scattered fishing and farming communities are so difficult that light aircraft are commonly used. The region has suffered badly from **depopulation** in recent years, as many of its people have now given up the battle to eke out a living from the harsh landscape and have migrated to Reykjavík. Nevertheless, the wild, uninhabited country of the Northwest Fiords is attractive to hikers in the summer months. Bird-watchers also like to visit the teeming sea-bird cliffs at **Látrabjarg**, the most westerly point in Europe, and **Hornstradir** in the north. The inhospitable climate, however, ensures that tourists are rare birds themselves!

TOP ATTRACTIONS

** **Reykholt:** associated with 13th-century statesman and writer Snorri Sturluson.
** **Sea-bird cliffs:** at Látrabjarg and Hornstradir in the Northwest Fiords.
** **Ísafjörður:** town with good fiord location and Iceland's best maritime museum.
** **Hraunfossar and Barnafoss Falls:** waterfalls in the upper reaches of the Hvítá valley.
** **Settlement Centre:** newly opened museum at Borgarnes, tracing the history of Icelandic settlement.

◀ *Opposite: Sugandafjörður, in the Northwest Fiords area of Iceland.*

WEST AND NORTHWEST ICELAND

CLIMATE

The weather in the southern part of the area differs little from that in Reykjavík, but the climate deteriorates to the north. The Snæfellsnes Peninsula juts out into the Atlantic and attracts a lot of wind and rain. Stykkishólmur has an annual **rainfall** total of 756mm (29.6in), a **January** average temperature of 1.8°C (29°F) and a **July** average of 10°C (50°F). The Northwest Fiord area experiences cold **Arctic winds** and heavy **snowfall** in winter, with Ísafjörður having an average temperature below freezing point for three months of the year.

▼ *Below: Inshore fishing boats. Most of the coastal villages in the northwest of Iceland depend on fishing for their income.*

HVALFJÖRÐUR AND BORGARFJÖRÐUR

North of Reykjavík, the Ring Road runs seaward around **Mount Esja**, some 918m (3012ft) high, before swinging around into **Hvalfjörður**. The name means 'whale fiord' and this was the centre of Icelandic whaling operations until the country's withdrawal from the industry in 1992. Whales are frequently seen in the fiord today and some 17 species have been recorded here. The deep waters of Hvalfjörður were ideal for British and American warships in World War II, and the remains of the base can be seen on the north side of the fiord. Equally unattractive is the ferro silicon smelter at Grundartangi, near the mouth of the fiord. On the north side is the delightful little church at **Saurbær**, built in memory of Hallgrímur Pétursson, who in the 17th century composed Iceland's best-known religious work, *50 Passion Hymns*.

Akranes ★★★

One of Iceland's largest fishing ports (population of just over 5500), Akranes is located right on the very tip of the peninsula which separates Hvalfjörður and Borgarfjörður. The town is dominated by the chimneys of its cement works, which uses local basalt and shell sand. Akranes can be reached by the new road tunnel across the mouth of

Hvalfjörður, which has cut the journey from Reykjavík by about 60km (37 miles), or alternatively by regular ferry services from the capital. The main attraction at Akranes is the **Regional Folk and Maritime Museum** (tel: 431 5566, open 10:00–17:00 daily, 13:00–17:00 in winter), just east of the town, at Garðar. There are indoor and outdoor exhibits, including *Sigurfari*, an old 19th-century decked cutter, and also numerous whaling artefacts. Outside the museum is a stone tower with inscriptions in both Icelandic and Gaelic. It was a gift from Ireland in 1974, commemorating the 1100th anniversary of the Settlement and Akranes's original Irish immigrants who founded the town around AD880.

Borgarnes ★★★

Situated halfway along the northern side of Borgarfjörður, Borgarnes is quite unusual in that it is perhaps the only coastal town in Iceland that doesn't specialize in fishing. Instead, it is a service centre for the inland area. Borgarnes has a small park, where there is a burial mound, said to be that of Skallagrímmur Kveldúlfsson, the father of Egill Skallagrímsson of *Egils Saga*

The West and Northwest Fiords

fame. It is said that Egill carried the body of his drowned son to be buried next to his grandfather – a touching tale that is depicted on a relief plaque made by the Danish artist Annemarie Brodersen. In 2006, the **Settlement Centre** was opened in some converted shoreside warehouses. It has two major exhibitions – The Settlement of Iceland and Egils Saga, with full audiovisual support (open 10:00–21:00 all year, tel: 437 1600, www.landnam.is).

Near to the Settlement Centre is **Puppet Theatre** (tel: 895 9447/894 3337, www.figurentheatre.is). Located in a line of restored 18th-century houses, the museum features puppets that bring to life the various Icelandic sagas.

THE UBIQUITOUS LUPIN

In mid-June the countryside is covered with wild flowers. One of the most noticeable is the **Alaskan Lupin** (*Lupinus nootkatensis*) which grows in blue swathes. This is no ordinary wild flower, for being a leguminous plant, it adds nitrogen to the soil. Its root system binds the soil together and helps to prevent erosion, which has proved useful on the *sandur* in south Iceland.

WEST AND NORTHWEST ICELAND

Reykholt ★★★

This small hamlet to the west of Borgarnes is one of Iceland's most important historical sites. It was the home of **Snorri Sturluson**, the famous 13th-century Saga writer and statesman. Snorri lived at Reykholt from 1206–1241 and wrote many of his best works here. Today, we can see the thermal pool where Snorri bathed and the nearby tunnel which connected with the farm where he lived. The tunnel probably led to the cellar where he was murdered by his enemies in 1241 at the age of 62. The modern church has a cultural centre where some of his work is on display. In front of the school is a statue of the writer by Norwegian sculptor Gustav Vigeland. It was a gift from Norway in gratitude for one of Snorri's most famous works, *Heimskringla*, a Saga featuring the kings of medieval Norway. In the cemetery of the older church is a gravestone marked *Sturlingareitur*, and it is possible that this might be Storri's last resting place. Also of interest in the Reykholt valley is the country's most powerful hot spring, known as **Deildartunguhver**. It spurts out water at 200 litres (352 pints) per second at a temperature of 100°C (212°F). Not surprisingly, a greenhouse industry has developed here and fresh produce is often on sale at the roadside. The hot water is piped some 60km (37 miles) to supply both Borgarnes and Akranes.

THE FORMIDABLE SNORRI

The life of the 13th-century Icelandic writer and diplomat Snorri Sturluson was as full of intrigue and violence as any of the Sagas. Born in 1179, he married an heiress at the age of 21, and liaisons with other wealthy women ensured that he became the richest man in Iceland. He mainly lived and worked on a large estate at Reykholt where he wrote his greatest works. He became law-speaker of the Alþing at the age of 36. He developed a close relationship with the King of Norway. Later that relationship soured and the King demanded Snorri's return to Norway. Snorri ignored his request and in 1241 he was assassinated at Reykholt by Gissur Þorvaldsson, a rival chieftain hoping to impress the King of Norway. Snorri left behind a formidable collection of literature, including the *Prose Edda, Heimskringla* and, in all probability, *Egils Saga*.

Inland from Reykholt ★

To the east of the Ring Road and to the west of the Langjökull icecap is an area, full of geological interest, which is known as **Húsafell**. It can also be approached by a scenic road from Þingvellir, though this route is only likely to be open during July and August. To the east of Húsafell are extensive lava sheets which include the **Hallmundarhraun Caves**. These feature a series of tubes within the lava; the longest, known as Surtshellir, is some 4km (2½ miles) in length. The caves have the usual stalactites and stalagmites, and occasional large caverns. Visitors should bring a torch, as there is no artificial lighting. West of Húsafell are the **Hraunfossar Falls**, where the glacial River Hvítá has created a gorge over 1km (0.6 mile) in length. The sides of the gorge have a long string of springs which emerge from the junction of porous rock and basalt. A track leads upstream to **Barnafoss** ('children's waterfall'), named after children who, while on their way to church, fell from a natural rock arch over the falls and were drowned.

THE SNÆFELLSNES PENINSULA

Running east–west and jutting out into the ocean, the Snæfellsnes Peninsula receives the full force of Atlantic gales. The population, not surprisingly, is sparse here. The south coast of the peninsula has a broad coastal plain, but lacks good harbours. Consequently there are no townships of any size, just a scattering of farmsteads. A mountain chain runs along the centre of the peninsula, rising to approximately 930m (3051ft) at **Tröllatindar**. The highest mountain, however, is **Snæfellsjökull**, at 1446m (4744ft), at the western end of the peninsula. It is a conically shaped dormant volcano with three distinct peaks, covered by a small icecap which can frequently be seen from Reykjavík, some 100km (60 miles) to the south. In Jules Verne's story *Journey to the Centre of the Earth*, the explorers began their journey at Snæfellsjökull, emerging sometime later at Stromboli volcano in Italy! Snæfellsjökull can be climbed by three different routes, which each take about four to five hours to complete and which demand the use of equipment such as crampons and ice axes. There are also snowmobile routes to the summit. Always be prepared for the worst possible weather.

◀◀ *Opposite: Snorri's Pool, Reykholt. Here the statesman and Saga writer Snorri Sturluson lived and died.*
▼ *Below: At Hraunfossar, a line of waterfalls emerges from a rock junction in the side of the gorge.*

WEST AND NORTHWEST ICELAND

▼ *Below: Sunset across
Breiðafjörður, a lovely wide
island-studded bay marking
the start of the Northwest Fiord
area. Ferries from Stykkishólmur regularly cross the bay.*

Stykkishólmur ★★★

The largest town on Snæfellnes Peninsula, Stykkishólmur
has a long history and many connections with the Sagas.
In the early days it was a religious centre. The nearby hill
of **Helgafell** (or Holy Mountain) has always been considered
to have supernatural powers and also figures strongly in
local folklore. Today Stykkishólmur is a trading and fishing port, specializing in shellfish. Close to the harbour is
a folk museum called the **Norwegian House**, which was
brought from Norway in 1828 by Árni Þorlacius (who also
made Iceland's first meteorological measurements at
Stykkishólmur in 1845). The museum is open Jun–Aug daily
12:00–17:00. Stykkishólmur's most striking building, however, is its new **Roman Catholic Church**. Built on a headland
and made of concrete, it soars skywards in gentle curves.

Also worth a visit is the new **Volcano Museum** in
Eldfjallasafn (tel: 433 8154, open May–Sep daily 11:00–
17:00). Located in an old cinema, the museum is largely
the work of retired vulcanologist Haraldur Sigurdsson.
The museum also organizes
local field trips.

The car ferry *Baldur*
makes regular trips from
Stykkishólmur across
Breiðafjörður to Brjánslækur
in the Northwest Fiords (tel:
433 2254, www.seatours.
is). Breiðafjörður is littered
with over 2000 small is-
lands, and the ferry stops at
one of these, named **Flatey**.
Once a religious and cultural
centre, few people live on
Flatey today, although many
city dwellers have holiday
homes here. The island
houses Iceland's smallest
and oldest library.

◀ *Left: Looking towards the Drangajökull icecap, showing a typical U-shaped glaciated valley.*

Elsewhere on the Snæfellsnes Peninsula ★★★

There are a number of other fishing settlements along the north coast of the peninsula. The most westerly is **Ólafsvík**, Iceland's longest established trading port, having been given its charter in 1687. There is a small folk museum based in an old packing house and an amazing church built without a single right angle. Further east is **Grundarfjörður**, surrounded by forbidding mountains. In the early 19th century it was used as a base by French fishermen, who built a church here. The northeastern part of the peninsula is marked by the broad **Hvammsfjörður**. The coastal village of **Búðardalur** is the main service centre for the region. Inland is the narrow **Laxárdalur Valley**, famous as the site of the *Laxdæla Saga*, a popular Icelandic love story. Several famous Icelanders were born in Laxádalur, including the writer Snorri Sturluson, the discoverer of America, Leifur Eiríksson, and the heroine of the *Laxdæla Saga*, Guðrún Ösvífursdóttir.

THE NORTHWEST FIORDS

Northwest Iceland is one of the most inhospitable parts of the country. Geologically, this is the oldest part of Iceland, with basalt rocks some 50 million years old. It was one of the most recent areas to be glaciated and has a large surviving icecap, called **Drangajökull**, which covers about 175km² (68 sq miles). The high interior, known as **Gláma**, is a tundra plateau, with thin rocky soil, moraines and lakes.

SORTING OUT YOUR GUILLEMOTS

Guillemots are easily recognized as black-and-white diving sea birds belonging to the **auk** family. They have a 'whirring' flight and an upright stance on land. In Iceland, however, identification is complicated by the fact that there are **three** species of guillemots. The most widely seen is the **common guillemot**, which is found throughout the northeast Atlantic. Rarer is the **black guillemot** which, as its name suggests, is black all over (except for white patches on its wings and bright red legs). The third species sends birdwatchers into raptures – this is **Brünnich's guillemot**, distinguished by a narrow white line stretching back from the eye and seen only with binoculars. The common and Brünnich's guillemots are cliff-nesters, but the black guillemot prefers bank holes.

WEST AND NORTHWEST ICELAND

▲ *Above: The small settlement of Mýrar, which nestles on the north side of Dýrafjörður.*
▼ *Below: The rugged scenery of the northwest highlands is formed by some of the oldest rocks in the country.*

The ice, which has only recently left, has carved out deep, steep-sided coastal fiords, making this region the most scenically attractive in Iceland. The climate, though, is harsh, with piercing Arctic winds and heavy snowfalls in winter. Farming is extremely difficult and many parts have become abandoned. Communications are problematic too. Remote from the Ring Road, northwest coastal roads are badly surfaced and wind around fiords, making journeys long and arduous. Public transport by road is infrequent, but there are a few ferries, particularly in Ísafjarðardjúp. The only sustainable work in the area is **fishing**. The warm Gulf Stream and cold Greenland Current meet offshore, providing good spawning conditions for fish. There are also sheltered harbours aplenty. Unfortunately, Government quotas on the fish caught have resulted in many fishermen leaving. There are, however, many attractions for the tourist in summer. For hikers, there are numerous marked trails amongst wilderness scenery, while for bird watchers, the northwest holds some of the finest sea-bird cliffs in the world.

FEATHERED NOMADS

One of the world's most remarkable nomadic birds, the **Arctic Tern** (*Sterna paradisæa*) is, in fact, very common in Iceland. The bird summers in northern sub-Arctic regions where it breeds, but in the northern winter it flies over 17,000km (10,500 miles) to the Antarctic. Arctic terns are regarded with special affection by the Icelanders, as their arrival is seen as the harbinger of spring. The birds can be less affectionate at their nesting sites, and will 'dive bomb' any intruders, including human beings, who are well advised to wear head protection.

Ísafjörður ★★★

The largest settlement in the Northwest Fiords area is Ísafjörður, which has around 4000 inhabitants. It has one of the most dramatic locations of any town in Iceland, situated on a narrow sand spit jutting out into the fiord, its steep sides cloaked with scree slopes and, at upper levels, hanging valleys left by glaciers. Ísafjörður has a long history as a trading port and today has an important fishing industry. It also acts as the cultural and commercial centre of the Northwest Fiords. Regular flights to Ísafjörður from Reykjavík have helped develop a modest tourist trade, but due to its remoteness and poor infrastructure, it will never be swamped with visitors.

A number of 18th-century wooden houses have survived on the end of the sand spit. Today these house the **Westfjörds Heritage Museum** which is full of old photographs, nautical artefacts and fishing implements. The star exhibit is a reproduction of an early six-oared sailing ship. Open mid-May–mid-Sep daily 09:00–18:00, tel: 896 3291.

There are several ferries which double as fiord sightseeing boats, including the *Fagranes*, which cruises the Ísafjarðardjúp, stopping on request. Its ports of call include the islands of Vigur and Ædey (Eider Island), both of which are noted for their bird life. *Fagranes* also visits **Hornstrandir**, in the northernmost tip of the Northwest Fiords. This wilderness area is now uninhabited and is designated as a nature reserve, typified by sheer sea cliffs, glaciated valleys and rugged mountains. The arctic fox thrives here, and whales and seals are often seen offshore. In the absence of grazing sheep, the wild flowers are spectacular. Most impressive of all are the sea-bird cliffs, which rise

◄ Left: An eider duck sits on her nest in the remote Dýrafjörður area of northwest Iceland.

▲ Above: The reflections of Dvergarsternsofell in the waters of Álftafjörður in northwest Iceland.

vertically in places to over 500m (1650ft). Guillemots, puffins, razorbills, kittiwakes and fulmars breed in profusion, while there is always the possibility of seeing the rare white-tailed sea eagle. Note that there is no accommodation in the Hornstrandir area apart from mountain huts.

An hour's excursion by boat from Ísafjörður leads to **Vigur Island**. In this pristine environment there are only 11 inhabitants, but thousands of tame seabirds nesting on the grassy slopes. There is a tea room, post office and the only eider duck feather factory in Iceland.

THE LAST HAUNTS OF THE WHITE-TAILED SEA EAGLE

The majestic white-tailed sea eagle once occurred all round the coast of Iceland and along its lakes and rivers. During the 19th century, however, numbers declined drastically as the eagle was persecuted by farmers who blamed it for killing lambs and taking eiders. Many of the birds were shot and others died after taking poisoned bait meant for foxes. In fact, the white-tailed sea eagle mainly takes dead lambs and can make little impression on the half a million eider ducks in the country. In 1913 a law was passed protecting the sea eagle, but it had little effect and by 1959 there were only 11 pairs in the country. There has been a gradual recovery in numbers, and there are now 30–40 breeding pairs, mainly in the Northwest Fiords.

Around the Northwest Fiords ★★★

Other coastal settlements of note include **Suðavík**, once a Norwegian whaling station, the geothermal centre of **Reykjanes**, and **Suðureyri**, which is in the unenviable position of having no direct sunlight for four months of the year. The most westerly point in Europe is marked by the lighthouse at **Látrabjarg**. To the south of this are the **Látrabjarg Cliffs**, which are 12km (7½ miles) long and rise to over 500m (1650ft). In summer the ledges of the cliffs teem with breeding sea birds, including puffins, guillemots, fulmars and cormorants. There is also an estimated one-third of the world's razorbills nesting here. The local people are accomplished at abseiling down the cliffs to collect birds' eggs, a skill that came in useful in 1947, when a British trawler ran aground at the foot of the cliffs. The local farmers casually saved the entire crew by hauling them up the 200m (650ft) cliffs by rope, even stopping halfway up, it is said, to give them soup!

BEST TIME TO VISIT

The south of this region can be visited for most of the year. The further north you go, however, the more hostile the winter climate becomes. The chilling Arctic winds and the poor surfaces of most of the roads in the Northwest Fiords area make this a **summer** venue.

GETTING THERE

The Ring Road goes through the southern part of this area, which is also well served by a number of scheduled bus routes. However, access is more difficult in the region of the Snæfellsnes Peninsula, and particularly in the Northwest Fiords. The ferry *Baldur* plies the route between Stykkishólmur on the Snæfellsnes Peninsula and Brjánslækur on the south side of the Northwest Fiords (tel: 433 2254, www.seatours.is). From there it is a circuitous drive to anywhere else in the area. Air Iceland flights run from Reykjavík to Stykkishólmur and Ísafjörður.

GETTING AROUND

Travelling in the Snæfellsnes Peninsula and the Northwest Fiords is difficult in winter when heavy snowfall can cause problems on the road. Many of the bus services in the region only run in summer, and even then careful planning is essential.

WHERE TO STAY

In the remoter areas of the west, few hotels are open all year, and in summer they can quickly become booked up. Forward planning is advisable.

Luxury

Hótel Búðir, 365 Snæfellsnes Peninsula, tel: 435 6700, www.budir.is Claims to be the only boutique hotel outside Reykjavík. A favourite haunt of Nobel prize winning author Halldór Laxness. Good views. Open all year round.

Mid-range

Hótel Borgarnes, Egilsgata 16, 310 Borgarnes, tel: 437 1119, fax: 437 1443, www.hotelborgarnes.com Closed in Dec, open in Jan and Feb for groups only; good restaurant.

Hótel Egilsen, Aðalgata 2, 340 Stykkishólmur, tel: 554 7700, www.egilsen.is Recently converted historic house close to the harbour. Good food and very welcoming.

Hótel Ísafjörður, Silfurtorg 2, 400 Ísafjörður, tel: 456 4111, www.hotelisafjordur.is Good restaurant. Cheaper annexe nearby. Open all year.

Budget

Budget accommodation available in hostels and camp sites. There are a number of **HI hostels** in the area, namely at Borgarnes, Grundarfjörður and Korpudalur Kirkjuból. There are several excellent **camp sites**, including those at Borgarnes, Ólafsvík and Ísafjörður.

WHERE TO EAT

High-class restaurants are somewhat few and far between in this part of the country, and frequently the restaurants in the hotels are the only available choice for dining. Particularly well recommended are the restaurant at the **Hótel Ísafjörður**, which has a very good tourist menu, and the one at the **Hótel Borgarnes**.

USEFUL CONTACTS

Tourist Information Centres:
Akranes: Suðurgata 57, tel: 433 1065/894 2500.
Borgarnes: Hyrnutorg, Borgarbraut 58-60, tel: 437 2214.
Stykkishólmur: Sports Centre, tel: 433 8120.
Ísafjörður: Aðelstræti 7, tel: 450 8060.
VisitWestfjords: the tourist office is at Árnagata 2–4, Ísafjörður, tel: 450 3002, and offers a variety of boat cruises and hiking excursions in the vicinity.

STYKKISHÓLMUR	J	F	M	A	M	J	J	A	S	O	N	D
AVE. TEMP. °C	-1.8	-0.7	-0.8	1.6	4.9	8.1	9.9	9.6	6.7	3.9	0.9	-0.8
AVE. TEMP. °F	28.7	30.7	30.5	34.9	40.8	46.6	49.8	49.3	44	39	33.6	30.5
AVE. RAINFALL mm	67.5	68.9	71.7	52.9	33.7	40.2	42.1	51.7	56.6	80.3	66.8	71.6
AVE. RAINFALL in	2.66	2.71	2.82	2.08	1.33	1.58	1.62	2.04	2.23	3.16	2.63	2.82

5
Northern Iceland

After the Reykjavík area, Northern Iceland is the part of the country which is most popular among tourists. It has many attractions, not the least of which is the weather. Despite being only a stone's throw away from the Arctic Circle (which straddles the offshore island of Grímsey), summers can be pleasantly warm and much drier than in the south of the country. Pastoral farming thrives in the lowland areas.

The coastline is marked by a series of rugged peninsulas protruding into the Arctic Ocean, with fiords, bays and occasional river deltas. Some of the inland areas have been heavily glaciated, leaving spectacular mountain scenery. The eastern part of the area lies on the plate boundary, and in the **Lake Mývatn** area there are numerous volcanic features, such as **Krafla** volcano, lava flows, pseudo craters and mud springs. In the extreme east is a largely unpopulated, gravel-strewn, cold desert, almost totally devoid of vegetation. Hikers head for the attractive **Jökulsárgljúfur National Park**, where a long gorge has been formed by glacial meltwaters. Numerous waterfalls can be seen here, including the imposing **Dettifoss**, said to be the most powerful falls in Europe. Bird-watchers are in their element in this part of Iceland, with Lake Mývatn a major attraction. Huge numbers of duck breed in this shallow lake, which is fed by warm underground springs.

The Ring Road bisects Northern Iceland and most of the important settlements can be found along its route. Dominating the area is **Akureyri**, the country's second

Don't Miss

*** **Jökulsárgljúfur National Park:** Iceland's own version of the Grand Canyon, with the powerful Dettifoss waterfall.
*** **Lake Mývatn Area:** teeming bird life and the country's most spectacular volcanic features.
*** **Glaumbær Folk Museum:** take a look inside a turf farm complex.
** **Húsavík:** superb whale-watching from this northern fishing port.
** **Goðafoss:** the accessible 'Waterfall of the Gods'.

◀ *Opposite: Turf huts at the Glaumbær Folk Museum to the south of Sauðárkrókur.*

NORTHERN ICELAND

largest town and the regional and service centre for the whole of Northern Iceland. It has an outpost of Reykjavík university, a clutch of interesting museums and some fine botanical gardens. It is also the main air and sea port of the area. A number of small fishing ports are scattered around the coastline, including **Húsavík**, which has become quite well known for its whale-watching tours.

▲ *Above: Whale-watching tours from Húsavík are likely to be rewarded with photographs such as this tail fin of a breaching sperm whale.*

THE WEST OF THE REGION

The Ring Road joins the area at the small settlement of **Brú** at the head of the narrow **Hrútafjörður**. This leads out into the wide bay of **Húnaflói**. The word translates as 'Bear Bay', named, no doubt, after the many Greenland bears which have washed ashore here on ice floes. The Ring Road now heads to the northeast, with distant views of the moraine-dammed salt-water lagoon of **Hóp**, where seals can often be seen basking on the sand at low tide.

The first settlement of any size is **Blönduós**, situated on both banks of the River Blandaá, a popular (and expensive) salmon river. Blönduós is dominated by its church – a modern concrete affair clearly designed in the shape of a volcanic crater. The only other features to detain visitors are a small **Textile Centre** (tel: 452 4300/894 9030)exhibiting local handicrafts and costumes, and the **Sea Ice Exhibition Centre** (tel: 452 4848), which looks at the effects that the weather had on early settlers. Don't miss the stuffed polar bear, who made a nuisance of himself when he washed up in the summer of 2008.

North of Blönduós is the rugged and remote **Skagi Peninsula**. The only settlement of importance here is the old trading centre and current fishing port of **Skagaströnd**. A gravel road runs around the perimeter of the peninsula. The northerly point is marked by an unmanned lighthouse, and nearby are some remarkable ledges of horizontal basalt.

From here the Ring Road heads inland over some superb

CLIMATE

The north of Iceland has a more continental climate than the south, with drier, sunnier summers, but colder winters and more snowfall. Rainfall is light, but northerly winds can bring very cold conditions. This is the most sunny part of the country, but the wind-chill factor is high. The temperature in Akureyri averages 2.4°C (27.5°F) in **January** and 10.7°C (51°F) in **July**, with an average total **rainfall** of 470mm (18.5in).

glacial scenery, before dropping right down into the Héradsvötn valley and the little settlement of **Varmahlíð**, which is currently growing as a service centre for the surrounding area.

Sauðárkrókur ★★★

Located at the head of Skagafjörður, Sauðárkrókur, with a population of around 2600, is the second largest town in the north of Iceland. Its position 25km (15.5 miles) north of the Ring Road means it doesn't see as many tourists as it deserves. The town developed on the site of an old trading post, and its industries include fish processing and the making of fibreglass. **Heritage House** (tel: 453 6870, open Jun–Aug, daily 12:00–19:00) has four old workshops – matchmakers, blacksmiths, saddlemakers and carpenters – brought from sites across the country. There are hiking possibilities in the mountains behind the town. Boat trips are offered to the island of **Drangey** (tel: 821 0090, www.drangey. net) in Skagafjörður, where the steep cliffs house thousands of breeding sea birds. Both the birds and their eggs have been a rich source of food for local people in the past.

THE ARCTIC FOX

Iceland's only native land mammal is the **arctic fox** (*Alopex lagopus*). Greyish brown in summer, in winter it grows a thick, furry coat that turns much lighter, almost white. It is well insulated and may even grow fur on its paws. The arctic fox was common throughout the country, but because farmers thought it killed lambs, it has been persecuted and has retreated to less habited areas. In fact, it poses little threat to healthy sheep and largely exists on small birds, eggs, fish and shellfish, though it will feed on carcasses of sheep and dead sea birds. There have been attempts to **breed** foxes on fur farms, but these animals have been brought in from abroad.

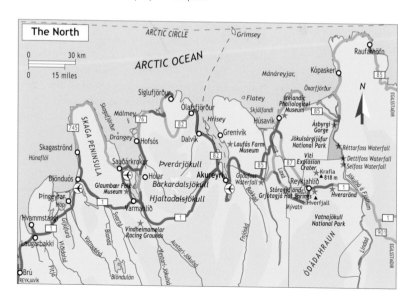

CONSERVATION AWARENESS IN ICELAND

It has to be said that conservation awareness in Iceland is low. Historically, the population has always been small and mainly confined to the coastal regions. There seemed little reason, therefore, to worry about the vast expanse of wilderness in the interior. The second half of the 20th century saw the growth of urban areas and the widespread use of four-wheel-drive vehicles, which gave the town-dwellers easy access to wilderness areas. Such regions are badly in need of protection. There are few voluntary environmental organizations, however, and conservation bills seem to attract little interest in the Icelandic parliament. Fortunately, it is gradually dawning on the authorities that Iceland has the potential to become one of the great **eco-tourism** destinations in the world. The sensitive sites, however, need protection.

South of Sauðárkrókur ★★★

The Héradsvötn River has built up a sizeable delta at the head of Skagafjörður. Although it is rich farmland, it is prone to flooding when snows melt in early summer. Above the flood plain to the west is the **Glaumbær Farm** (tel: 453 6173), based on an 18th-century turf farm. It consists of a complex of small separate buildings linked by a central passageway. The buildings include guest rooms, a dairy, a pantry, a kitchen and living rooms (or *baðstofa*). It was in the latter that the work of the farmhouse took place. The women of the house would weave and spin, while the men combed wool and made ropes. A member of the household would usually read a Saga or recite poetry while the others worked. The *baðstofa* also contained beds, and many people would sleep together for warmth. The rooms are full of fascinating artefacts from previous centuries. There is also a blacksmith's forge: a forge has existed here since the 11th century when the first farm was founded. Glaumbær is also the burial place of Snorri Þorfinnsson, who is believed to have been the first European to be born in North America. This was in the year 1003, when his parents went on an expedition to Vinland. The museum, which is open mid-May–mid-Sep daily 09:00–18:00 and by appointment all year, is highly recommended. There is a small café in a nearby building.

Iceland horse enthusiasts will certainly wish to visit the **Vindheimamelar Racing Grounds**, approximately 10km (6 miles) south of Varmahlíð. An audiovisual presentation is followed by a demonstration of the five gaits of this hardy breed. Refreshments are provided, but reservations are necessary.

Hólar ★★★

Another diversion to the north of Varmahlíð along the eastern side of the Heraðsvötn valley eventually leads to the religious centre of Hólar. This was the northern bishopric in Iceland from 1106 until the Reformation. The first wooden cathedral here was built from Norwegian timber, and for a century it was the world's largest wooden church. In 1798, the bishop's seat was abolished, and the site later became an **agricultural college**. The present church at Hólar dates from 1757 and is made of the local red sandstone. The bell tower contains the remains of the first Bishop, Jón Ögmundarson who, together with his son, was executed at Skálholt for his opposition to Danish reforms. The interior of the church is full of interest and well worth a visit. Climb the tower for spectacular views. There are guided tours between 09:00 and 18:00 daily.

AKUREYRI

Located at the head of Eyjafjörður, the fast-growing town of Akureyri is the 'capital' of Northern Iceland and one of the country's most pleasant urban areas. Akureyri became a trading centre in the early 17th century, but it was over 100 years later that the first people lived here. Its main growth has taken place during the 20th century. It now has a population of around 18,000. Akureyri has always specialized in fish products, and herring salting was initially important. After the stocks declined, the emphasis turned to the canning and freezing of larger fish such as cod. Other industries include food processing, brewing and, increasingly, tourism. A number of old wooden buildings have been preserved in the town, and its residents take great

◄ *Left: Icelandic horses show their paces at the Vindheimamelar Racing Grounds.*
◄◄ *Opposite: The Glaumbær Folk Museum is on an 18th-century turf farm.*

THE REMARKABLE ICELANDIC HORSE

Despite the small size of the Icelandic horse, please don't ever call it a pony! It is a **purebred** horse, found in a variety of colours, and unique in having **five gaits**. In addition to the usual walk, trot and gallop, it has the tölt and the pace, the latter two giving a smooth, comfortable ride for the equestrian. This singular horse is a valuable animal and is exported throughout the world. A hardy animal, it is also a good **workhorse**, and up to the start of the 20th century it was essential for transport and farm work. Furthermore, its toughness meant that it was quite happy to spend the winter outdoors. Today, the Icelandic horse is largely used for **sport** and **recreation**.

▲ Above: The harbour at Akureyri, where there is an important fish canning and freezing industry.

pride in their gardens, which means that the town has a pleasant cared-for feel. There is an attractive central shopping mall and numerous bookshops, libraries, churches and museums. The riverside is full of interest, with fishing and cargo boats, families of harlequin and eider ducks, and planes flying low down the fiord to land at the airport.

Akureyrarkirkja *

The parish church sits high on the hill overlooking the town centre and is well worth the climb. This modern church has rather a 'geological' appearance, and it is not really surprising to learn that it was designed by the same architect who was responsible for the Hallgrímskirkja in Reykjavík. It is worth looking at the interior – the central chancel window came from the old Coventry Cathedral in the UK, somehow surviving the blitz. The ship hanging from the ceiling is an old Norse tradition meant to protect seafarers.

Museums ***

Akureyri has an extraordinary number of museums. Many of these are small affairs celebrating former sons of the town and will be of minimal interest to the foreign visitor, but others are well worth a visit.

The fascinating **Akureyri Folk Museum** displays a collection of household and workplace artefacts dating back to the time of the Settlement. Situated at Aðalstræti 58, this museum is open Jun–mid-Sep daily 10:00–17:00, and Thu–Sun 13:00–16:00 at other times.

Nonnahús, located at Aðalstræti 54, is the childhood home of the Reverend Jón Sveinnsson (1857–1944), who was nicknamed 'Nonni'. He wrote a number of works for children, based on his own youthful experiences. The building is a revealing example of the cramped conditions people lived in during the 19th century in Iceland. Sveinsson's statue dominates the garden. The house is open Jun–Aug daily 10:00–17:00, Sep–May by appointment only (tel: 462 3555).

Laxdalshús, at Hafnarstræti 11, is the oldest building in Akureyri, dating from 1795. It functioned originally as a Danish trading house. It is no longer open to the public.

There are also small museums celebrating the work of Davíð Stefánsson and Matthías Jochumsson, both of whom became Icelandic poets laureate.

Visitors arriving by air could check out the **Icelandic Aviation Museum** at Akureyri Airport (tel: 461 4400, open Jun–Aug daily 11:00–17:00, Sep–May Sat 14:00–17:00 or by appointment). Icelandic aviation history is detailed and there are a number of restored aircraft.

Visitors should not leave Akureyri without visiting the **Botanical Gardens**. The gardens were founded in 1912 by the local townswomen and were then taken over by the local authority in 1955. There is a comprehensive collection of Icelandic plants, all carefully labelled, plus a number of different plants from all around the world. It is amazing to find Mediterranean plants surviving at this high latitude. The Botanical Gardens are open daily 08:00–22:00 (weekends 09:00–22:00), tel: 462 7487.

AKUREYRI'S FAVOURITE SON

The Reverend **Jón Sveinsson** (1857–1944), who was also known as 'Nonni', lived in Akureyri as a child before being educated in France, Denmark and England. He was ordained as a **Jesuit priest** and taught in Denmark for many years, but ill health forced him into an early retirement and he turned to writing **children's stories**, many of which referred back to his own childhood in Iceland. He wrote in German, but his books have been translated into nearly 50 different languages. Many of his original works can be seen in his former home, **Nonnahús**, in Akureyri.

▼ Below: Akureyri Church, designed by the architect responsible for the Hall-grímskirkja in Reykjavík.

NORTHERN ICELAND

NORTH OF AKUREYRI

There are a number of small ports north of Akureyri. On the
eastern side of Eyjafjörður is **Grenivík**, which has a large fish-
freezing plant. Just to the south is the **Laufás Farm Museum**,
based on an old turf farmhouse dating from 1850. Open Jun–
Aug 09:00–17:00, tel: 463 3196. On the opposite side of the
fiord is the ferry port of **Dalvík**. Its main claim to fame is the
1934 earthquake which measured 6.3 on the Richter Scale
and destroyed half the town. Ferries leave Dalvík for Grímsey,
calling en route at the island of Hrísey in the middle of the fiord.
Further north is the port of **Ólafsfjörður**, which is considered to
have one of the most attractive settings in the country. It
is now reached by a 3.5km (2-mile) tunnel through the
surrounding peaks. At the northern end of the peninsula lies
the fishing port of **Siglufjörður**, located in a short but spectacular fiord. It was originally named Thormóðseyri after Thormóður
the Strong, who was the first settler. Siglufjörður was the third
largest town in Iceland during the years of the herring boom.
The town declined with the herring, but the golden years are
remembered in the harbourside Herring Museum. Open Jun–
Aug daily 10:00–18:00, Apr, May, Sep daily 13:00–17:00. At
other times by appointment, tel: 467 1604.

Goðafoss ★★★

The Ring Road leaves Akureyri eastwards and follows the far
shore of the fiord, giving superb views across to the town. It

then climbs the mountains through superb glacial scenery before dropping down into the next valley, that of the River Skjálfandaflót. Just a short stroll from the road is Goðafoss, Iceland's most accessible **waterfall**, formed as the river cuts into a lava field. The name means 'Waterfall of the Gods', a title which dates back to AD 1000 when the law-speaker, Þorgeir, was returning from the Alþing. The parliament had just decided to adopt the Christian religion, and Þorgeir decided that the falls would be a good place to dispose of his pagan idols.

Húsavík ★★★

From the road junction at nearby Laugar, Route 845 leads northwards to the busy **fishing port** of Húsavík. Situated on an attractive harbour and backed by snow-capped mountains, Húsavík has a population of around 2500 and is the main service centre for northeast Iceland. Húsavík's first inhabitant was a Viking named Garðar Svavarsson. He gave up and left after the first winter, but two of his slaves were unfortunately left behind. In reality, these were Iceland's very first settlers, but they are never credited as such. Today Húsavík makes its living mainly from fish processing, sulphur exports and tourism. In recent years the town has become Iceland's most important **whale-watching centre**. Over 90% of trips record minke whales, while other cetaceans commonly seen are humpbacks, fins, sei and orcas, plus harbour porpoises and dolphins. Before you go on a whale-watching trip, it is worth paying a visit to the **Whale Museum** (tel: 414 2800,

◄ *Left: Goðafoss is Iceland's most accessible waterfall.*
◄◄ *Opposite: The northern fishing port of Húsavík is the whale-watching capital of Iceland.*

THE GOÐAR AND THE FALLS

Way back in the year 1000, the 'goðar', or pagan chieftains, had a heated debate at the **Alþing** about whether to abandon paganism and adopt Christianity. The decision was finally left to the **law-speaker**, Þorgeir Þorkelsson. He is said to have curled up under his sheepskin in a booth at Þingvellir for three days and nights while he considered the problem. He finally came up with a classic compromise, deciding in favour of Christianity, but allowing the people to practise paganism in the privacy of their homes if they so wished. To set a good example, Þorgeir, on his way home, threw his pagan effigies into the waterfalls — thereafter to be known as the 'Waterfall of the Gods', or **Goðafoss**.

NORTHERN ICELAND

▲ Above: Húsavík's distinctive church, built with timber brought from Norway.

www.whalemuseum.is). Open Jun–Aug 08:30–18:30 daily, Apr, May & Sep 09:00–16:00 daily, Oct–Mar 10:00–15:30 Mon–Fri (closed 12:00–13:00). Located in an old harbourside slaughterhouse, the museum charts the history of whaling and more recent conservation measures. It is difficult not to be impressed by the huge whale skeletons.

The **Town Museum, Safnahúsið**, is also worth a visit. As well as the usual social memorabilia, there is also a stuffed polar bear, which was washed up on the island of Grímsey and greeted with a bullet. Open Mon–Fri 13:00–18:00, Sat 13:00–16:00, tel: 453 6640.

There are two islands in Skjálfandi Bay, namely **Flatey** and **Lundey**, which are easily reached by boat from Húsavík. The latter is particularly noted for its large colony of puffins.

GRÍMSEY

Some 41km (25 miles) north of the mainland is the island of Grímsey. Covering an area of 5.3km² (2 sq miles), it straddles the Arctic Circle (visitors can obtain documents certifying that they have crossed over into the Arctic). Only 120 people live on the island, mainly around the harbour at Sandvík. Ferries and planes connect Grímsey to the mainland, especially in the summer months. Most visitors are bird-watchers. The cliffs teem with sea birds during the breeding season, with guillemots, puffins, razorbills, fulmars and even a few pairs of the rare little auk.

LAKE MÝVATN AREA

This is one of the most important tourist locations in Iceland, currently receiving an estimated 100,000 visitors a year. Apart from the lake itself, which attracts bird-watchers from all over the world, there are a host of volcanic features to observe. The climate, too, is agreeable as the area is in the rain shadow of the Vatnajökull icecap, making it one of the driest parts of the country.

Lake Mývatn ★★★

The lake, which sits on the Mid-Atlantic Ridge, covers around 37km² (14 sq miles). It is essentially a shallow lake, with an average depth of 2.5m (8ft). This means that light can penetrate right to the bottom, making it rich in vegetation and nutrients, which in turn prove attractive to wildfowl. The numbers of ducks present in the summer are staggering, with probably around 50,000 pairs and 15 species represented. These include tufted duck, wigeon, mergansers, long-tailed duck, teal, gadwall and goosanders. Add to this list whooper swans, slavonian grebe, red-necked phalarope, skuas, terns, snow buntings and snowy owl, and it is clear why birders flock here in huge numbers. European bird-watchers in particular are keen to see American species such as Barrow's goldeneye and harlequin duck (which breeds along the River Laxa).

A metalled road runs along the east of the lake and a dirt track follows the western side. A large area in the northwest of the lake is a protected nesting area and out of bounds for much of the summer. Although much of Mývatn ices over in winter, part of the northern section is fed by hot springs and remains ice-free, so that there are wildfowl present throughout the year. Bird-watchers and other visitors should beware of insects. Mývatn means 'lake of the midges' and there are swarms of these little pests, especially on calm days in the

PSEUDO CRATERS

A feature of the Mývatn area is the large number of **islands** in the lake (about 50) and the numerous small hills in the vicinity. On inspection they are seen to have concave summits and are described by geologists as **pseudo craters**, largely because no lava ever flowed out of them. They were formed when lava flowed across the lake. The trapped water boiled and exploded through the lava, building up cones and craters. They vary in size from 3m (9ft) to 250m (820ft) across.

▼ *Below: The shallow waters of Lake Mývatn teem with a variety of wildfowl.*

▶▶ *Opposite: Remnants of winter ice in the Viti explosion crater and lake situated on the slopes of the frequently active Krafla.*

summer. Net head covers are recommended.

The lake contains over 50 islands, most of which are **pseudo craters**. They look like mini volcanoes, but were in fact formed by gas explosions. This gives a hint of the **volcanic features** which abound in the area, particularly to the northeast of the lake. There has been continual volcanic activity since the end of the Ice Age. Particularly significant were the '**Miýatn fires**' which flowed from the Krafla area between 1724 and 1729 along a fissure which is still occasionally active. More recent were the '**Krafla fires**' in the early 1980s. Subterranean rumblings suggest that more volcanic activity is imminent. Many of the volcanic features can be viewed at first hand.

Sigurgeir's Bird Museum, Ytri-Neslönd, Mývatn, is a superb ornithological museum beside the lake. Open mid-end May daily 12:00–17:00, Jun–late Aug daily 09:00–18:00, late Aug–Oct daily 12:00–17:00, Nov–mid-May daily 14:00–16:00, tel: 464 4477.

BIRD-WATCHERS' PARADISE

Lake Mývatn is renowned for its birds. The bridge over the **River Laxa** in the southwest corner of the lake is claimed to be one of the prime bird-watching spots in the world. The abundant wildfowl feed largely on midges and their aquatic larvae. Practically every Icelandic breeding bird is found in the area, besides cliff-dwelling sea birds. The summer months are the most rewarding and few birders will leave disappointed.

Dimmuborgir ★★

Dimmuborgir, which can be translated as 'black castles', is an area of lava located on the eastern side of the lake. Thought to be around 2000 years old, the lava here is believed to have been dammed by older material and then forced up into a wide variety of contorted shapes. It is possible for visitors to wander around among the lava pillars, caves and holes, which are now developing some interesting vegetation. To save the area from human erosion, set walking routes have been roped off – but it is still quite possible for people to get lost!

Lake Mývatn

Hverfjall ★

Just north of Dimmuborgir stands
the cinder cone of Hverfjall which
rises to 163m (534ft). It was
formed during a cataclysmic
eruption around 2500 years ago.
It is possible to walk up the steep
path to the rim of the large crater,
though hikers are no longer allowed
to descend to the crater floor.

Hot Springs ★

Situated between Hverfjall and the village of Reykjahíð are
a couple of popular hot springs which give visitors an
opportunity for bathing. The first, **Stóragjá**, is hidden in a
crevice and has to be reached by means of a rope ladder,
but the second, **Grjótagjá**, is much more accessible and is
divided into separate sections for men and women. The
water temperatures are generally around 47°C (116°F),
but are cooling annually.

Krafla ★★★

To the northeast of the lake is the impressive Krafla
volcanic complex. It is readily accessible, with visitors able
to drive there directly from the Ring Road, passing the Krafla
Geothermal Power Station en route. Krafla itself does not
resemble the archetypal cone-shaped volcano, but is in
fact a reasonably level system of fissures, along which the
surface occasionally swells and erupts. Nearby, however, is
the dramatic **Viti explosion crater**. Viti is the Icelandic name
for 'hell' and the 320m (1050ft) wide crater, which often fills
with ice floes in the winter, certainly fits the description.

Hverarönd ★★★

About 6km (3.7 miles) to the east of the lake, at the side of
the Ring Road and situated on the Mid-Atlantic Ridge, is the
hill known as **Námafjall**. Among its cracks and fissures are
bands of yellow sulphur. The mineral was once mined here,

COPING WITH THE MIDGES

One of the less appealing
aspects of Lake Mývatn is the
swarms of midges which gave
the lake its name. They hatch
between June and August and
can make life very unpleasant.
They seem particularly
attracted to the **carbon
dioxide** on people's breath and
seem intent on entering the
nose, eyes, ears and mouth.
They are particularly active on
calm days and reduce in number
the further you are from the
lake. Insect repellent and net
headware are strongly recommended. The good news is that
the midges do not bite (although
the blackfly certainly does – it
can be readily identified by its
buzzing noise). Midges are
eagerly devoured by wildfowl
and fish. In fact, the Laxa
River is reputed to have the
country's biggest salmon as
a result of this.

NORTHERN ICELAND

but was not commercially successful. Beneath the hill is the remarkable
area of **Hverarönd**, undoubtly one of
Iceland's most unforgettable sights.
There are bubbling mud pools, steam
vents, hot boiling springs, fumeroles
and the distinctive stench of sulphur
everywhere. Visitors are advised to
stick to the roped-off paths as some
of the surface material is fragile.

▲ *Above: Part of the lava flow
that threatened the church at
Reykjahlíð in 1929.*
▶▶ *Opposite: Dettifoss is
claimed to be Europe's most
powerful waterfall in terms of
water volume.*

Reykjahlíð★★★

This is the only settlement of any size in the Mývatn area.
Though originally merely a farmhouse, it has grown in size
with the development of tourism and is now an important
service centre for the surrounding region. There is a church,
hotel, supermarket, tourist office, bank and small museum.
The original church was threatened by the 1929 lava flow
which completely destroyed many of the buildings in the
village, but miraculously the flow passed by a few metres
from the church. A modern church was built on the site in
1972 and is well worth a visit.

The Reykjahlíð area has seen a number of industrial
ventures, some of which have been successful, others spectacular failures. The main employer at the moment is the
Bjarnarflag **diatomite plant**, which is fortunately well away
from the lake. Diatoms are microfossils which are dredged
up from the lake bed. After treatment they are used as a filler
in such products as paint and toothpaste. The diatomaceous
ooze is moved by pipeline to the refining plant just north of
the Ring Road. There are environmental questions about the
effect the dredging is having on the ecology of the lake, and
naturalists are particularly worried about operations moving
to other parts of the lake. Though diatomite mining is highly
successful, the **Krafla Geothermal Power Station** has been a
dubious operation and its drilling is believed to have set off
the Krafla eruptions in the mid-70s. Before leaving the area,
take a look at the land on the opposite side of the road to the

DIATOMS

The bed of Lake Mývatn has
a layer of diatomaceous ooze
which is up to 15m (49ft)
thick. Diatomite is the skeletal
remains of diatoms, which are
microscopic single-cell **algae**.
The fossil shells are one ten-
thousandth the size of a grain of
sand and consist largely of silica.
The diatomite is sucked up from
a barge and pumped by pipeline
to the processing plant, where
it is dried using steam from the
nearby Bjarnaflag geothermal
power station. The result is a
white powder which is packed
and transported to Húsavík, from
whence it is **exported** to Europe
for use as a filler in a variety of
industries.

diatom plant. This is marked by a pipe with steam bursting out of it and was the site of a drill hole to ascertain the feasibility of locating a geothermal power station here. Just by its side is an underground bread oven. Peer through the glass doors to see the *hverabrauð* taking 24 hours to bake.

JÖKULSÁRGLJÚFUR NATIONAL PARK ★★★

Jökulsárgljúfur was given its national park status in 1978. It is essentially a 30km (19-mile) canyon formed by *jökulhlaup*, or glacial meltwater floods. The canyon is drained by the River **Jökulsá á Fjöllum**, which rises on the Vatnjökull icecap and then flows north for 206km (128 miles) to the Arctic Ocean. Jökulsárgljúfur is often described as 'Iceland's Grand Canyon' and although its measurements cannot compare with the American giant, it is certainly an impressive sight. The main part of the canyon averages 100m (328ft) in depth and has a width of 500m (547yd). There is a series of impressive waterfalls, including Hafragilsfoss, Dettifoss and Selfoss. Of these, **Dettifoss** should not be missed, as it is claimed to be Europe's most powerful waterfall. Although only 45m (148ft) in height, it dispatches some 500m^3 (17,658ft^3) of water per second – a truly awesome sight. Downstream from here is another extraordinary landform, detached from the main canyon and known as **Ásbyrgi**. It is a dry, horseshoe-shaped gorge, which the Vikings believed was the hoofprint of Odin's horse.

The geographical explanation is that it is an incised abandoned meander, left high and dry when the Jökulsá á Fjöllum changed its course during a *jökulhlaup*. Fulmars breed on the walls of the gorge in summer. The national park is wonderful for hiking, but there is no formal accommodation within the park, and just two official camp sites. The national park brochure indicates the main walking trails.

THE SNOWY OWL

Few sights are more evocative of Iceland than the flight of the white, ghostly snowy owl. This magnificent bird is **diurnal** and largely solitary. It can often be seen sitting upright on a low eminence, surveying the surrounding land for prey. It is resident in Iceland, but has become **extremely rare**, being largely confined to the more inaccessible areas – although some have been seen in the Mývatn area in recent years. Snowy owls usually prey on ptarmigan, but will take young ducks and goslings in the breeding season.

NORTHERN ICELAND

Best Time to Visit

As with most parts of the country, the **summer** months from June to September are the most convenient times to visit the north of Iceland. At this period the area is drier than it is in the south, and it also has more sunny days. At this northerly latitude there is scarcely any night at all during the summer.

The **winter** months are not recommended for visitors, due to the heavy snowfall, the cold blasts of wind from the Arctic, and the lack of daylight, particularly during the months of December, January and February.

Getting There

The Ring Road is usually kept open during winter, but may be temporarily closed from time to time during heavy snowfalls until the snow can be cleared from the road. Akureyri is approximately 390km (242 miles) by road from Reykjavík. BSÍ coaches take the better part of a day to cover this distance (tel: 562 1011, www.bsi.is). It is much quicker to reach the northern parts of the country by air. Air Iceland operates daily flights from Reykjavík to Akureyri, and less regular flights from Akureyri to Egilsstaðir, Grímsey, Ísafjörður and the Westman Islands.

Getting Around

The Ring Road is very well surfaced throughout the north of Iceland, and cars have no problems during summer. However, four-wheel-drive vehicles are generally recommended for travelling here in winter. The main settlements in the area are all linked by bus, but away from the Ring Road bus services may be confined to one or two ser-vices a day. Cars and four-wheel-drive vehicles may be hired in Akureyri and in Sauðárkrókur.

Where to Stay

There is no accommodation in the international luxury range in northern Iceland. There are, however, several comfortable hotels in the mid-range.

Mid-range

Hótel Kea, Hafnarstræti 87–89, 600 Akureyri, tel: 460 2000, fax: 460 2060, www.keahotels.is Situated in the shadow of the church, this hotel has all the facili-ties, but on a busy road.

Hótel Reynihlíð, 660 Reykjahlíð, Mývatn, tel: 464 4170, www.reynihlid.is The accommodation price includes a continental buffet breakfast.

The Edda Group runs a number of hotels in the area; some are summer hotels. They are found at Laugarbakka and Akureyri, www.hoteledda.is

The Foss Group have hotels at Laugar, Dalvík and Húsavík. Some are summer hotels, www.fosshotel.is

Húsavík Cape Hotel, Laugarbrekka 16, tel: 463 3399, www.husavikhotel. com Excellent views over the town and bay which are a short walk away.

Hótel Varmahlíð, 560 Varmahlíð, tel: 453 8170, www.hotelvarmahlid.is Modern hotel right on the Ring Road. Best restaurant in the area.

Budget

Guesthouse Akurinn, Brekkugata 27A, Akureyri, tel: 461 2500. Basic, but good value.

Árból Guesthouse, Asgarðsvegur 2, 640 Húsavík, tel: 464 2220. Plain bedrooms and shared bathrooms. Friendly owners. Open all year.

Gistiheimilið Hraunbrún, Reykjahlíð, tel: 464 4103. This is a good centre for the Mývatn area. Next to the campground.

Hrafninn Guesthouse, Brekkugötu 4, Akureyri, tel: 463 2300. Close to the bus station and centre of town.

Youth Hostels can be found at Akureyri, tel: 462 3657; at Ósar (near Hvammstangi in the west of the region), tel: 862 2778; and at Sæberg, near Brú, tel: 894 5504.

Camping

Two camp sites in the Jökulsá National Park, three at Mývatn, others at Akureyri,

Blönduós, Goðafoss, Húsavík, Sauðárkrókur and Ólafsfjörður. These are all official seasonal sites.

WHERE TO EAT

The best restaurants in the north of the country are invariably those in hotel dining rooms, and in the more remote areas these are often the only option in the evenings. Hotel restaurants, however, are usually rather expensive. There are a few other restaurants in the larger settlements which can be recommended:

Sauðárkrókur
Mid-range
Kaffi Krókur, Adalgata 16, Sauðárkrókur, tel: 453 6299. This is a cosy restaurant in the heart of the town, serving Icelandic food in a cosmopolitan setting.

Akureyri
Mid-range
Bautinn, Hafnarstræti 92, tel: 462 1818, www.bautinn. is Here, mountains of food are to be had at bargain prices, served in an atrium-like setting.
Greifinn, Glerágata 20, tel: 460 1600. This restaurant serves moderately priced Icelandic food as well as a selection of burgers, pizzas and pasta.

Mývatn
Mid-range
Gamli Bærinn, Reykjalid,

tel: 464 4170. This restaurant serves an excellent meal of the day packed with local specialities, including the cake-like *hverabrauð*.

Húsavík
Mid-range
Gamli Baukur, tel: 464 2442. Well-cooked fresh fish in a popular wooden harbour-side restaurant.

Budget
Cheaper options are found at **snack bars** attached to service stations, which usually have a filling tourist menu.

TOURS AND EXCURSIONS

Many tours and excursions around the popular venues in the north can be booked in Reykjavík, but a number of local firms can arrange tours for small groups, particularly for adventure trips.
Hestasport-Activity Tours, located at the Vindheimamelar racing grounds 20km (12 miles) south of Varmalið. Raftahlið 20, 550 Sauðárkrókur, tel: 453 8383, www.riding.is Arranges riding tours (long and short) and whitewater rafting trips as well as trips to experience the autumn

rettir (sheep round-ups).
Nonni Travel, Brekkugata 5, Akureyri, tel: 461 1841, arranges excursions to Hólar and Grímsey by ferry and by air. This company also offers excursions in the Mývatn area amongst many others. For whale-watching tours from Húsavík, contact **North Sailing**, on the harbourside, tel: 464 7272. They use traditional Icelandic oak boats.

USEFUL CONTACTS
Tourist Information Centres are situated at all the major settlements in the north. The most important one is in **Akureyri**, Hof Culture House, Strandgata 12, tel: 450 1050, website: www.visitakureyri.is It is open Jun–Aug week-days from 09:00–21:00, weekends from 12:00–20:00. Also Sep–May week-days from 08:30–17:00. Other Tourist Information Centres can be found at: **Blönduós**, situated at the campground, tel: 452 4520; **Varmahlið** and **Sauðárkrókur**, at the Minjahús Exhibition Centre, tel: 455 6161; **Mývatn**, at Hraunvegur 8, tel: 464 4390; and **Húsavík**, at the Whale Museum, Hafnarstétt 1, tel: 464 4300.

AKUREYRI	J	F	M	A	M	J	J	A	S	O	N	D
AVE. TEMP. °C	-2.2	-2.6	-2.6	0.7	7.2	9.9	12.5	10.5	6.3	3.7	1.7	-0.5
AVE. TEMP. °F	28	27.3	27.3	33.3	44.9	49.8	54.5	50.9	43.3	38.6	35	31.1
AVE. RAINFALL mm	55.2	42.5	43.3	29.2	19.3	28.2	33	34.1	39.1	58	54.2	52.8
AVE. RAINFALL in	2.17	1.67	1.7	1.15	0.76	1.11	1.3	1.34	1.54	2.29	2.14	2.08

6
East Iceland

Remote from the Mid-Atlantic Ridge, East Iceland is the country's geologically most stable and oldest area. It consists largely of basalt, a rock which flowed large distances from long-lost volcanoes. The whole area was later **glaciated**. Moving down from corries high in the mountains, the glaciers gouged out deep, U-shaped valleys, which were later flooded – in the post-glacial rise in sea level – to form today's impressive **fiords**. The Ring Road from Mývatn in the north to Egilsstaðir passes through one of Iceland's most majestic features: a **cold desert**, which is almost completely devoid of vegetation. The southwest boundary of the region is marked by the edge of **Vatnajökull**, Europe's largest icecap, from which numerous **glaciers** run down to the coastal plain.

The main service and transportation centre for the area is the rather unremarkable town of **Egilsstaðir**, which is located in the **Largafljót Valley**. The river here flows through **Lake Lögurinn**, which is 100m (330ft) deep. It is also Iceland's longest lake and reputedly has a resident monster. The slopes of the valley are clothed with the country's largest and most mature forest, which has a network of footpaths for exploring the woods. Each fiord has a small fishing port, the most important of these being **Seyðisfjörður**, **Djúpivogur** and **Reyðarfjörður**. Further to the south is the sheltered port and communications centre of **Höfn**, the first major settlement on the Ring Road since Selfoss, approximately 400km (250 miles) away to the west.

Don't Miss

*** **The Cold Desert:** the fascinating mountain desert in the rain shadow of the Vatnajökull icecap.
** **The Eastern Fiords:** a region of fishing villages and lovely Scandinavian-style wooden buildings.
** **Lake Lögurinn:** a deep ribbon lake, reputedly with its own resident monster.
** **Petra's Rock Museum:** Petra Sveinsdóttir's private collection of rocks, minerals and fossils, displayed in her house and garden.

◀ *Opposite: The ptarmigan, Iceland's most common game bird. Many are taken annually by gyrfalcons.*

EAST ICELAND

It is claimed that the
Eastern Fiords have Iceland's
most agreeable climate. Sitting
in the rain shadow of the
Vatnajökull icecap, the
rainfall is low by Icelandic
standards. **Summers** are
sunny and mild. **Winters** can
be wet, but snow is only
heavy on the mountains, and
the area is protected from
cold Arctic winds.

A HIGHLY PRIZED FALCON

Europe's largest falcon is
the magnificent **gyrfalcon**,
and Iceland is one of its
strongholds. Specially protected, around 200 pairs
remain, scattered around the
country wherever its main
prey, the ptarmigan, is found.
For many centuries, the
gyrfalcon was one of Iceland's
most valuable exports, as it
was highly prized for falconry
and hunting. It is estimated
that during the Middle Ages
over 200 birds were exported
annually. Falconry still exists in
many countries in the world and
there is an illicit smuggling trade
in gyrfalcon chicks and eggs.
Gyrfalcons usually nest on cliff
ledges, often in an old raven's
nest, if necessary evicting the
ravens first.

Seyðisfjörður is Iceland's only car ferry link with Europe. From the ferry port, drivers once had to take the northerly route to Reykjavík via Mývatn, but in 1974 the Ring Road was completed. This allowed cars to take the southerly option, cutting both time and distance considerably. Few motorists stop for long in the eastern fiords region, with the result that it has none of the usual trappings of tourism, thus adding to its attractions for the discriminating visitor.

CROSSING THE DESERT

The route between Mývatn and Egilsstaðir crosses an interior cold desert which is one of the most fascinating parts of the country. The Ring Road, which is largely surfaced by gravel in this region, passes bare plains covered with volcanic ash and the glacial deposits of occasional meltwater floods. It climbs remote rocky passes and bridges rushing streams, with hardly a single item of vegetation to be seen. On a fine day, the journey is full of interest, but in the mist and rain, it can have a brooding, rather sinister atmosphere. Surprisingly there are two small isolated areas of farming here. At the northern end of the road, close to the Jökulsá á

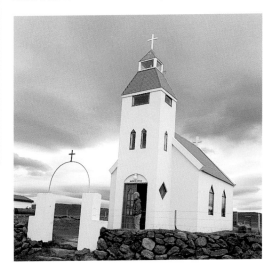

▶ *Right: The tiny church
at Mödruðalur, built by a local
farmer in memory of his wife.*

Fjöllum River, is the remote farm of **Grímsstaðir**. The road here was once crossed by ferry, and the old ferry-man's hut, reputed to be haunted, can still be seen in the distance. Further south is the little oasis of **Möðrudalur**. At 469m (1539ft), this is almost certainly the highest farm in the country. Buses stop here for half an hour or so, to allow passengers to use the snack bar and toilets.

It is worth strolling over the road to see a small church, built by the local farmer in 1949 in memory of his wife. Note its unconventional altarpiece. This particular stretch of the Ring Road gives excellent views of **Herðubreið** (the name means 'broad-shouldered'), a plateau-like mountain capped with a volcanic cone. Composed of palagonite, it rises to a height of 1060m (3478ft) and dominates the surrounding area. The Ring Road then crosses a high pass capped with cairns, which are said to mark the boundary of the bishoprics of Hólar and Skálholt, before dropping down into the valley of the **Jökulsa á Dal.**

Eastern Iceland

▲ *Above: East Iceland is the most likely part of the country to spot small herds of wild reindeer.*

EGILSSTAÐIR

Originally just a farmstead on the eastern bank of the Lagarfljót river, Egilsstaðir has grown rapidly with the completion of the Ring Road and the development of air travel, so that it is now the transportation and service centre for the whole of eastern Iceland. It has a population of around 1600 and, despite its rather sterile look, it makes a good centre for exploring the surrounding area. There is little to see in the town itself, apart from the modern geological theme **church** and a **folk museum** which also includes a restored farmhouse. The folk museum is being refurbished. For opening times ask at the local TIC or tel: 471 1412 or visit www.minjasafn.is The River Lagafljót, which is about 140km (87 miles) long, is Iceland's second longest river. Its murky glacial floodwaters are crossed by one of the country's longest bridges, some 310m (339yd) in length, which links Egilsstaðir with the altogether more attractive village of **Fellabær** on the western bank.

Around Egilsstaðir ★★★

To the north of the town, Route 94 leads to the bay of **Héraðsflói**, where the Jökulsa á Dal and Lagaflót rivers form a delta, with marshes and coastal sand dunes. At the farmstead of **Húsey** there is a youth hostel. This is an excellent bird-watching area, particularly for waders and geese.

South of Egilsstaðir, the river flows through **Lake Lögurinn** (or **Lagarfljót**). This long, deep ribbon lake is reputed to have a resident monster (Lagarfljótsormurinn or Lagarfljót Worm). It is possible to circumnavigate the lake by road, although some of the surface is composed of gravel. The eastern shores of the lake are clothed with some of Iceland's most

THE MONSTER OF THE DEEP

Many of the deep glaciated ribbon lakes of the world, probably not coincidentally, have stories of resident monsters. Despite state-of-the-art, high technology research at many sites, nowhere has the presence of a 'monster' been conclusively proven. Lake Lögurinn, to the south of Egilsstaðir, is no exception. Despite centuries of rumours of the existence of a dragon-like creature, there is no hard evidence available. Nevertheless, in a country in which a survey of over 50% of the population showed a lack of denial over the existence of elves, anything is possible!

mature trees, one rising to the princely height of 15m (50ft)! This is excellent walking country, with its many hiking trails and picnic sites. Further trails to the south of the lake lead to the waterfalls of **Hengifoss** (Iceland's third highest) and **Lagarfoss**, the latter of which has a small power plant and a fish ladder for migrating salmon. A further track, accessible by four-wheel-drive vehicles, leads to a boggy moorland and the extinct volcano of **Snæfell**. At 1833m (6014ft), it is the highest mountain in the country outside the icecaps. It is also as good a place as any in Iceland for seeing wild reindeer.

THE EASTERN FIORDS

Though lacking the rugged grandeur of their counterparts in the northwest of Iceland, the Eastern Fiords are scenically one of the most pleasant areas of the country. The fiords are generally aligned east–west, so that the settlements are usually on the north (south-facing) sides of the water, to receive the maximum benefit of the sun. There is a string of small fishing ports, which gained considerable prosperity in the days of the herring boom, so that their wooden houses have a wealthy Scandinavian feel about them. Despite having a reputation for the best weather in Iceland, few tourists stay in this area for long. Those that do stay have the benefit of missing the crowds.

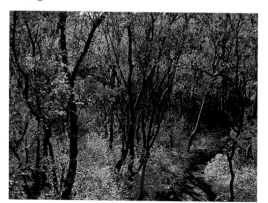

REFORESTATION

On the eastern bank of Lake Lögurinn lies the **Hallormsstaðarskógur**, Iceland's largest area of forest. Over 50 varieties of trees are seen here, mainly types of conifer, birch and poplar. This has been the headquarters of the **State Forestry Service** since 1907. They have searched the world for species which will survive in Iceland's harsh climate. It is quite probable that Iceland was covered with trees in the days of the Viking settlement, but that they were quickly removed for fuel and building material, and regeneration was prevented by sheep grazing. Today, there are a number of organizations throughout the country, in both rural and urban areas, engaged in planting trees, using the advice of the State Forestry Service.

◀ *Left: Trees on the State Forestry Service's land on the eastern bank of Lake Lögurinn, near Egilsstaðir.*

EAST ICELAND

Borgarfjörður Eystri ★★★

Due north of Egilsstaðir, and reached by way of Route 94 and the stunning mountain range of **Dyrfjöll**, is the small village of Borgarfjörður Eystri (shown on some maps as Bakkagerði). This was the home of Iceland's best-known landscape artist, **Jóhannes S Karvel**. The village church has an altarpiece painted by Karvel, representing the Sermon on the Mount.

Seyðisfjörður ★

Due east of Egilsstaðir and connected by Route 93 is the **ferry port** of Seyðisfjörður. For many people this will be their first glimpse of Iceland – and they are rarely disappointed. It sits at the head of a narrow curving fiord backed by snow-capped mountains. The attractive harbourside buildings are made of wood, all mainly constructed by a Norwegian entrepreneur in the middle of the 19th century, when it was an important trading port. The *Norröna* ferry, operated by Smyril Line, runs a scheduled service throughout the year, connecting Seyðisfjörður with the Faroe Islands, Shetland, Norway and Denmark.

Neskaupstaður ★

The next settlement is **Neskaupstaður** which, with a population of over 1600, is the largest town in East Iceland. Owing to its remote position, it is bypassed by most tourists. In fact, it was not linked to the rest of the country by road until 1947. Today, its economy is largely involved in fish-related industries. Just to the southwest is the fishing and trading port of **Eskifjörður**, backed by the attractive mountain Hólmatindur which rises to some 985m (3231ft). The town is mainly noted for its **Maritime Museum** (tel: 470 9063, open 13:00–17:00 Jun– Aug). Housed in a 19th-century warehouse, it is filled with fishing and whaling artefacts. In the hills behind the town is an old Iceland Spar mine which, although it is now closed down, was once the world's biggest producer

▼ *Below: The garden of Petra's Stone Museum at Stöðvarfjörður.*

of this mineral which was a vital component of early microscopes.

Reyðarfjörður ★★★

This town is located at the head of the fiord of the same name, in the midst of rich farmland. Reyðarfjörður was an important Allied base during World War II, and a **Museum of War Memorabilia** opened here in 1995, where the visitor can learn about the military occupation of Reyðarfjörður during the Second World War and its impact on the Icelandic people. Open Jun–Aug daily 13:00–17:00 or by appointment, tel: 470 9063. The Ring Road reaches the coast near Breiðalsvík. Reyðarfjörður is the site of the Fjardaál aluminium smelter whose construction, in the late 2000s was highly controversial. Power is supplied by the Kárahnjúkar hydroelectric power plant whose construction involved the submerging of a vast beautiful landscape under a reservoir. The debate over clean energy versus nature, and also the import of many foreign labourers led to heated debates. It is worth visiting the small fishing village of **Stöðvarfjörður** just to see the amazing **Rock Museum** (tel: 475 8834, www.steinapetra.com). Situated in a private house, it is the personal collection of Petra Sveinsdóttir. Rocks, fossils and minerals seem to fill every corner, along with the odd stuffed bird and ancient household artefact. Open May–Sep daily 09:00–18:00.

Djúpivogur ★

Of the remaining fishing villages, only Djúpivogur is of interest. It is located on a headland on the southern side of Berufjörður and backed by the pyramid-shaped Búlandstindur, which rises to 1090m (3576ft). Djúpivogur was an important **Danish trading station** as far back as the 16th century, and some of the oldest houses in the town today were built by Danish merchants. The *Löngubúð* warehouse on the harbourside has been restored and is now the **local museum and art gallery**. Just offshore is the island of **Papey**, which was once a hermitage for Irish

▲ *Above: The harbour at Djúpivogur. An old warehouse in the port has been converted into an interesting folk museum.*

THE YULETIDE LADS

As Christmas approaches, Iceland's version of Santa Claus puts in an appearance. These are the **Yuletide Lads**, or *jólasveinar*. In the country's folklore they were child-eating ogres who descended from the mountains in groups of 13, in homespun clothes, to play pranks on people. Nowadays, influenced by the commercial Father Christmas image from other parts of the world, the Yuletide Lads have adopted the red garments and long white beards of the traditional Santa Claus. An Icelandic horse, however, is more likely to pull their sledge than a red-nosed reindeer.

▲ *Above: Numerous glacier tongues run down from the Vatnajökull icecap.*

monks, until they fled at the arrival of the Norsemen. Today the island is uninhabited, apart from its seals and sea birds. Cruises run from Djúpivogur to Papey during the summer months.

Höfn ★★★

The Ring Road skirts the first of the *sandur* which mark the southern side of the Vatnajökull icecap. The main town and **port** of this stretch of the coast is Höfn. The name means 'harbour', and its pronunciation can best be described as a 'hiccup'. Located on Hornafjörður, which is in fact a bay that is almost completely enclosed by two spits, the narrow entrance calling for skilful navigation.

The completion of the Ring Road has boosted Höfn's **population**. Fishing, farming and tourism are the main sources of employment.

There is a **Nautical Museum** in an old warehouse close to the sea, a reminder of the town's fishing history. Open Jun–Aug daily 08:00–20:00, tel: 478 1540. It is also hoped to open a further museum covering local folk history, local wildlife ecology and an exhibition on glaciers in the near future. Ask at the TIC for details.

Höfn is also the main centre for arranging tours to the **Vatnajökull icecap** and to the **Jökulsárlón Glacial Lagoon** (*see* chapter 7 for information on both). There are icecap tours available by snowmobile, and also by glacier buggy, skiddoo and by ski. However, visitors are warned not to venture out on to the icecap independently, but to use the expert guides that are available and take their advice regarding equipment and clothing.

PTARMIGAN

The ptarmigan is Iceland's only game bird and is seen throughout the highland areas of the country. It is essentially a bird of the tundra and feeds mainly on the shoots of heather, crowberry and bilberry. The ptarmigan has the ability to moult three times a year to adapt to changing environmental conditions, so that it may be pure white in the winter snows, but a patterned grey-brown during the summer. Camouflage is the ptarmigan's main form of defence, and the female sitting on eggs is almost impossible to spot. Its main predator is the gyrfalcon, which can reduce the ptarmigan's numbers by as much as a third in a season.

Best Time to Visit
The **summer**, June–August, is the best time, particularly if arriving by car ferry from the Faroes, Scandinavia and Scotland. The eastern fiords have the most favourable climate, and here the visiting season can be extended into May and September.

Getting There
This is the only part of Iceland that can be approached by **ship** from abroad. The ferry *Norröna*, run by the Faeroese Smyril Line (tel: 298 345 900, www.smyril-line.com) operates a weekly service all year linking Seyðisfjörður with Esbjerg in Denmark, Bergen in Norway, Tórshavn in the Faroe Islands, and Shetland. The **road** route to the area is via the Ring Road; the southern route is quicker and shorter than the northern. Bus services connect the main towns on the Ring Road. **Air Iceland** runs services to Egilsstaðir from Reykjavík, Akureyri and Ísafjörður.

Getting Around
Apart from a private **car**, the only option for getting around the region is by **bus**. There are services daily around the Ring Road, but routes linking the fiord ports are less regular. Be prepared for a reduced timetable in winter.

Where to Stay
There are no hotels in the luxury range, but plenty of choice in the other categories.

Mid-range
Hótel Höfn, 780 Hornafjörður, tel: 478 1240, fax: 478 1996, www.hotelhofn.is Also has a cheaper annexe.
Hótel Snæfell/Hótel Adlan, (three old buildings housing hotels under the same management) Austarvegur 3, 710 Seyðisfjörður, tel: 472 1460, fax: 472 1570, www.hotelaldan.com Harbourside hotel convenient for ferry.
Hótel Capitano, Hafnarbraut 50, Neskaupstað, tel: 477 1800, www.hotelcapitano.is Housed in a 100-year old corrugated iron clad building on the sea front.
Hótel Framtíð, Vogaland 4, 765 Djúpivogur, tel: 478 8887, fax: 478 8187, www.hotelframtid.com Overlooks the harbour; good restaurant.
The **Edda Group** has hotels at Egilsstaðir, Hallormsstaður and Höfn, tel: 444 4000; and the **Foss Group** at Lindarbakki and Höfn, tel: 478 2555.

Budget
Guesthouse Skipalækur, Fellabær, tel: 471 1324. Sleeping bag accommodation and some lakeside chalets.
Youth Hostels at Höfn, Reyðarfjörður and Seyðisfjörður, tel: 575 6700, www.hostel.is

Camping
Camp sites at Borgafjörður, Egilsstaðir, Neskaupstaður, Eskifjörður, Reydarfjörður, Breiðdalsvík and Höfn.

Where to Eat
Good restaurants are scarce outside hotel dining rooms, but most service station snack bars serve a good tourist menu.

Budget
Café Nielsen, Tjarnarbraut 1, Egilsstaðir. tel: 471 2626. Summer only, but superb menu.

Tours and Excursions
Visiteast, Tjarnarbraut 39e, Egilsstaðir, tel: 470 3860, www.east.is offers boat trips on Lake Lörgurinn.
Tanni Travel, tel: 476 1399, arranges hikes around the Snæfell area and buggy trips on Vatnajökull.
Papeyjarferðir, tel: 478 8838, runs cruises in summer from Djúpivogur to Papey.
In Höfn, **Vatnajökull Tours**, tel: 478 1000, run snowmobile and jeep tours on and around Vatnajökull.

Useful Contacts
East Iceland Information Centre, Tjarnarbraut 39e, Egilsstaðir, tel: 470 2320, www.east.is
Höfn, tel: 470 8330.

EGILSSTAÐIR	J	F	M	A	M	J	J	A	S	O	N	D
AVE. TEMP. °C	0.3	0.6	0.1	1.4	3.3	6.2	8	8.3	6.6	4.5	1.8	0.6
AVE. TEMP. °F	32.5	33	32.2	34.5	37.9	43.2	46.4	46.9	43.9	40.1	35.2	33
AVE. RAINFALL mm	134	103	116	87	93	87	97	114	180	169	129	121
AVE. RAINFALL in	5.28	4.05	4.57	3.42	3.66	3.42	3.82	4.49	7.09	6.66	5.08	4.77

7
South Iceland

The central part of South Iceland is dominated by the huge mass of the **Vatnajökull icecap**, which is Europe's largest ice sheet and the third largest in the world. Iceland's highest mountain, **Hvannadalshnjúkur** at 2119m (6952ft), pokes its head above the ice. Vatnajökull National Park has now been extended and claims to be the largest in Europe. **Glaciers** snake their way down from the icecap, most prominently in a southerly direction. Lurking under the ice are several **volcanoes**, such as **Grimsvötn**, which periodically erupt and melt large quantities of ice, causing glacial floods or *jökulhlaups*. As well as causing widespread damage, these *jökulhlaups* have built up huge spreads of sand and gravel known as *sandur*. It was these *sandur* which prevented the completion of the Ring Road until 1974. Only after this date was the south central part of Iceland opened up for tourism.

Just to the southwest of Vatnajökull is a smaller icecap, **Mýrdalsjökull**, which also has a subglacial volcano, **Katla**. Here, again, there is a *sandur* to the south. The area around the icecaps has a wealth of places for tourists to visit and few fail to be impressed with **Jökulsárlón**, a glacial lagoon where calving icebergs can be viewed from a boat. **Skaftafell**, Iceland's largest national park and the second to be proclaimed, is also popular with visitors and offers good hiking possibilities amongst stunning scenery. Snowmobile and ice-buggy trips on the two icecaps are another favourite tourist activity. Waterfalls abound, including the impressive **Svartifoss** (named after its black lava columns) and

Don't Miss

*** **The Icecaps:** try a snowmobile or glacier buggy ride on Vatnajökull or Mýrdalsjökull.
*** **Jökulsárlón Lagoon:** take a boat trip among the icebergs.
*** **The Interior:** cross the wild and uninhabited interior by four-wheel-drive vehicle.
*** **Skaftafell National Park:** attractive area with a variety of scenery and wildlife.
** **The Coast around Vík:** cliffs, stacks and beaches, full of breeding sea birds.
* **The *Sandur*:** huge sand and gravel plains deposited by glacial floods.

◄ *Opposite: Skógafoss, one of Iceland's most impressive waterfalls.*

SOUTH ICELAND

▲ *Above: Svínafellsjökull, in the Skaftafell National Park.*

CLIMATE

The climate of south Iceland differs little from that of the Reykjavík area to the west, except that there is heavier snowfall on the higher land, the icecaps and the interior. The snow ensures that the tracks through the interior are only open for around two months of the year. On the coastal plain the rainfall is moderate to heavy for much of the year. The Skaftafell area, situated in the shelter of Vatnajökull, has a sunnier microclimate. Vík receives an annual rainfall of around 2300mm (91in), with an average **January** temperature of 0.9°C (33.6°F) and an average **July** temperature of 9.7°C (49.5°F).

Skógafoss. There are several places of interest for bird-watchers. The *sandur* contain Iceland's largest concentration of skuas, while the cliffs and stacks at **Dyrhólaey** have a good selection of breeding sea birds, including puffins and guillemots.

The coastline of this region is somewhat featureless, and it is one of the few parts of the Icelandic coast with no fishing ports. There are few settlements of any size at all. The only coastal town in the area is **Vík**, while the sole settlement between Mýrdalsjökull and Vatnajökull is the former religious site of **Kirkjubæjarklaustur**. In the western part of the region are the largely modern towns of **Hvolsvöllur** and **Hella**, located in the middle of an area that is rich in associations with the *Njáls Saga*.

THE VATNAJÖKULL AREA ★★★

The facts and figures applied to the Vatnajökull icecap are impressive in themselves. It is Europe's largest ice-sheet and the third largest in the world (after Antarctica and Greenland). It covers an area of 8538km² (3296 sq miles), which is approximately 8% of Iceland. Its central plateau lies around 1500m (4922ft) above sea level, with fringing *nunataks* (mountain peaks protruding above the ice) such as **Barðarbunga**, at 2009m (6592ft), and **Hvannadalshnjúkur**, which at 2119m (6952ft) is Iceland's highest mountain. It is estimated that the icecap is over 1000m (3281ft) thick in places. Whereas the Ice Age ended around 8000BC in most parts of Europe, the base of the ice on Vatnajökull dates from the start of the 1st century AD. Because of the high precipitation in the area and the fact that the accumulation of snow in winter is greater than the rate of melting in summer, the ice has built up rapidly. On the other hand, global warming has led to the retreat of the glacier snouts over the last two decades, leaving meltwater lakes between terminal moraines and the ice front. These features can easily be seen on **Kvíájökull**, **Fjallsjökull** and **Svínafellsjökull**, three glacial tongues just to the northwest of Höfn. Vatnajökull National Park takes up 13% of the country's landmass and now incorporates Deltifoss and the entire Vatnajökull icecap.

Owing to the dangerous conditions on Vatnajökull, excursions are best confined to organized tours. The usual route to the icecap is from the Ring Road up a track to the Skálafellsjökull mountain hut. Here, opportunity to sample glacier buggies and snowmobiles abounds. There are also cross-country ski options.

Jökulsárlón ★★★

Many visitors vote Jökulsárlón to be the highlight of their Icelandic experiences. It is an impressive glacial lagoon located at the snout of Breiðamerkurjökull glacier, which calves off icebergs into the lake. These icebergs are varied in colour – some white, some blue, others black or striped with volcanic ash. As they melt, they crack and crash around. The whole lagoon is incredibly beautiful and the icebergs

> ### THE VATNAJÖKULL GLACIER BURST
>
> In September 1996, the **Grímsvötn** subglacial volcano on Vatnajökull erupted, sending a column of steam over 10,000m (33,000ft) into the sky. The magma melted the ice, forming a huge subglacial lake. Just over a month later the waters of the lake rose and drained in a massive glacial burst, or *jökulhlaup*, causing an estimated 3000 billion cubic litres of water to pour down onto the coastal plain within a few hours. The protective dykes proved useless and some 1200m (3500ft) of Ring Road bridges were destroyed. Believed to have been Iceland's fourth largest volcanic eruption this century, it was seen on television screens throughout the world.

The South and the Interior

SOUTH ICELAND

The Vatnajökull glaciers have some fine examples of moraines. These are ridges of boulders and rock 'flour' which have been eroded by glaciers on their slow passage downslope and eventually re-deposited. **Terminal moraines** are found across the snout of a glacier. If the glacier then retreats, a **moraine-dammed lake** may result. **Lateral moraines** are found along the sides of glaciers, while **medial moraines** are seen on the ice in the centre of the glacier (usually formed from lateral moraines after two glaciers have merged). Both lateral and medial moraines are temporary features, as they are destroyed by meltwater.

can be viewed at close hand from an amphibious boat. Seals occasionally pop up their heads as the boat drifts past. The lagoon was used for several scenes in the James Bond film *A View to a Kill*. All the service buses that travel along the Ring Road stop at the lake, where there are toilets, a restaurant and a camp site. It is well worth walking from the lagoon to the sea. The lagoon is drained by the **River Jökulsá** (almost certainly Iceland's shortest glacial river), which runs under the suspension bridge carrying the Ring Road before reaching the sea about 200m (220yd) or so away. Icebergs are quite frequently washed down the river and many of them become stranded on the beach, where they gradually melt away, forming curious shapes in the process.

Sandur Country ★★

A few kilometres west of Jökulsárlón, the first of the *sandurs* are encountered. These desert-like areas are plains of gravel and sand interspersed with a host of ever-changing braided streams. Much of the material is deposited during glacial bursts, or *jökulhlaups*. The largest of the *sandur* is **Skeiðarársandur**, which is fed from the Skeiðarárjökull glacier.

The *sandurs* have always presented problems for transport, and it was not until 1974 that the Ring Road was completed in this area. Even so, the road can be temporarily put out of use after a *jökulhlaup*, such as the one which occurred in 1996.

◄ *Left: Svartifoss (Black Falls), named after the dark columns of basalt that occur on either side.*
◄◄ *Opposite: Melting icebergs assume these strange shapes in the Jökulsárlón glacial lagoon.*

SKAFTAFELL NATIONAL PARK ★★★

Tucked into a sheltered south-facing lobe of the Vatnajökull icecap is Iceland's largest National Park, Skaftafell. In terms of visitor numbers it is one of the most popular locations in the country. Founded in 1967 (as a joint venture between the government and the World Wildlife Fund), the park covers 1600km² (618 sq miles). It includes such diverse landscapes as ice sheet, glaciers, tumbling glacial rivers, waterfalls, luxuriant vegetation and moorland. Add a variety of bird life and abundant wild flowers and Skaftafell's popularity is understandable. It also has the benefit of a superb micro-climate, situated as it is in a sheltered sunny position.

Skaftafell has a number of good hiking trails, the most popular of which is to the **Skaftafellsjökull glacier**, the snout of which is black with rubble and volcanic material. This takes around two hours return, but there are many hikes of longer duration with marvellous views of the glacial features. Another attraction is the **Svartifoss** waterfall, named after the black basalt columns along the lip of the falls and the valley sides, which are said to be the inspiration for many public buildings around the country. Svartifoss is reached by the path from

CROSSING THE *SANDUR*

One of the most formidable tasks for travellers in Iceland has always been crossing the *sandurs* – the outwash plains of sand and gravel deposited in glacial bursts. It was not until 1974 that the Ring Road was completed by bridging some of the larger streams on the *sandur* to the south of Vatnajökull. During the summer months, storms can be caused by the descending movement of cold air from the icecap. The resulting wind-blown sand can do considerable damage to the bodywork of cars. At such times, motoring organizations suggest putting a cardboard sheet across the radiator grill to protect the engine. Attempting to cycle across the sandur in these conditions can be sheer misery.

▲ *Above: Iceland's most popular camp site, in the Skaftafell National Park.*

the campground. Allow 1½ hours for the return walk. It is also worth continuing along the track to the west of the falls to **Sjónarsker**, a prominent rock with a viewing disc, giving panoramas towards the *sandur* and the coast. Skaftafell is of great interest to wildlife enthusiasts. Over 200 species of plant have been recorded here, while trees include rowan, birch and willow, some of which are quite tall (in Icelandic terms). Many of the typical highland bird species are found here, including golden plovers, redwings, ptarmigan, snipe and meadow pipits, all of which breed in the park.

Park Practicalities

Skaftafell is very accessible, being so close to the Ring Road, and the BSÍ Reykjavík–Höfn buses also stop here. The park's facilities include a car park, camp site, service area with restaurant, coffee shop, supermarket and an information centre. Detailed maps of the park are available in the shop. Skaftafell's popularity, however, comes with a price. On summer weekends it can become extremely crowded, and the noisy camp site has been likened to a 'tented refugee site'.

WEST OF SKAFTAFELL

The Ring Road at this point crosses the northern side of Skeiðarársandur. After about 35km (22 miles), the little hamlet of **Núpsstaður** is reached. Backed by the steep cliffs of Lómagnúpur, which rise to 767m (2550ft), the settlement of Núpsstaður was once an ecclesiastical centre. All that remains today is a collection of working farm buildings plus a delightful turf-roofed church. Made of stone and wood, the church dates from 1756 and is probably the smallest place

SAFETY ON THE ICECAPS

Nature rules on the Icelandic icecaps, and the country's history is full of examples of accidents and tragedies which have befallen foolhardy travellers. Heavy snow, strong winds and whiteouts can occur at any time, even in summer, and crevasses can be deep and treacherous. Experts suggest that no climbing should take place at all in winter. Visitors in summer should be well equipped, know the routes, check the prevailing conditions and be aware of how to contact the rescue services in case of an emergency. Better still, go on a professionally led tour.

of worship in Iceland. It was restored in the 1930s, and services are still held annually on the first Sunday in August. The key can be obtained from the farmhouse.

Klaustur ★★★

The only settlement of any size between Vík and Höfn is the unpronounceable **Kirkjubæjarklaustur**, generally known as 'Klaustur'. The modern appearance of this village belies its fascinating history. It was first inhabited by Irish monks before they were driven away by the Vikings. Later, in 1186, a Benedictine convent was established here, but it was disbanded in the mid-16th century during the Reformation. This may not have been a bad thing, as two of the nuns are said to have been burnt at the stake – one for criticizing the Pope and the other for sleeping with the Devil! In 1783 Kirkjubæjarklaustur was threatened by lava from the Laki eruptions (a series of fissures to the north of the village). The local priest, Jon Steingrímsson, is reported to have assembled all the inhabitants in the church and delivered a 'fire and brimstone sermon'. When the service was over, the congregation went outside only to find that the lava had miraculously been diverted past the village. A modern **Steingrímsson Memorial Chapel** was built in 1974, on the site of the original church, to commemorate the priest's *eldmessa*, or 'fire sermon'. One strange feature which should not be missed is the **Kirkjugólf**, a more or less flat rock surface covering some 80m² (280ft²). This was always thought to be the floor of an old church, which was reasonable considering the ecclesiastical background of the area. It is now known, however, that this is an entirely natural feature – the smoothed upper surface of a series of basalt columns. Kirkjubæjarklaustur today has a small airstrip and acts as a

▼ Below: Hexagonal blocks of basalt at Klaustur, once thought to be the floor of an old church.

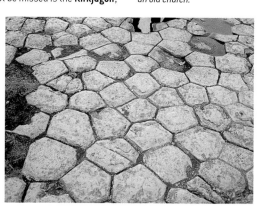

SOUTH ICELAND

LAKI AND THE HAZE FIRES

The most disastrous volcanic event in Iceland's recorded history is without doubt the **Laki eruptions of 1783**. Today Laki is an extinct row of cones and craters just to the west of Vatnajökull, and may be connected to the subglacial Grímsvötn volcano. When Laki erupted in 1783, it is estimated that some 90 billion tonnes of lava were ejected, destroying large areas of farmland and killing half the country's livestock. **Smoke** from the eruption affected the climate for many years and some 9000 people died in the so called 'haze famine' which followed.

▼ *Below: The small regional centre of Vík. Its black sand beach, pounded by the Atlantic waves, has a breeding colony of rather aggressive Arctic terns.*

service centre for the surrounding farming community, as well as making a good base from which to explore the area.

VÍK Í MÝRDAL ★

At the eastern end of the *sandur* is Vík, the southernmost town of mainland Iceland and also, reputedly, the rainiest. Once a fishing port, the town abandoned this activity during the 19th century as it lacked a harbour. It is now a service and transport centre. An attractive town of some 400 inhabitants, Vík has the Mýrdalsjökull as a backdrop, with the steep-sided, flat-topped headland of Reynisfjall to the west. To the east stretches a beach of black volcanic sand, pounded by huge North Atlantic waves. This was the only non-tropical beach to be listed by the US magazine *Islands* as one of the Top Ten in the world. However, this is definitely not a beach for sitting on, not only because of the weather, but because of the colony of aggressive Arctic terns who resent human interference at breeding time.

In Vík itself there are few sites to visit, except perhaps the delightful church occupying a dominating clifftop position. Boat trips, in an amphibious vehicle, run to the sea-bird cliffs in summer, but calm seas are essential for the cruises to operate.

Hekla
▲
1491 m

Fjallabak
Nature Reserve

● Hella

Hvolsvöllur

Seljalandsfoss
Waterfall

Eyjafjalla-
jökull
▲1666 m

Mýrdalsjökull

Katla▲
1306 m

Skógafoss
Waterfall ● Skógar

ᴦHeimaey

● Vík

Dyrhólaey

ATLANTIC OCEAN

Along the Coast ★★★

Just offshore from Vík are the photogenic black sea stacks of **Reynisdrangar**. Both the stacks and the headland are filled with breeding sea birds during the summer months, including razorbills, fulmars, guillemots and a large colony of puffins. On the far side of Reynisfjall is another headland called **Dyrhólaey**. It is 120m (390ft) high and incorporates a natural arch, through which small boats can pass during calm weather. Nearby is the large shallow lagoon of **Dyrhólaós**, another good bird-watching site. Away to the northwest is the hill of Pétursey, about 275m (900ft) high, which was an island before it became surrounded by glacial deposits.

◀ *Left: The distinctive sea stacks off the coast of Vík have breeding colonies of sea birds such as fulmars and guillemots.*

MÝRDALSJÖKULL ★★★

Mýrdalsjökull is one of Iceland's major icecaps. It is the fourth largest in size, covering some 700km² (270 sq miles) and reaching 1480m (4855ft) in height. Like the larger Vatnajökull to the east, it receives high precipitation, up to 8000mm (315in) annually, so that the accumulation of ice has been significant, reaching a depth of over 1000m (3281ft). Like Vatnajökull, it also has a subglacial volcano, **Katla**, which has erupted 16 times since Iceland was settled. Each *jökulhlaup* has deposited great quantities of sand and gravel, so building up the **Mýrdalssandur**, which covers some 70km² (27 sq miles). The Katla *jökulhlaups*, when in full flow, are estimated to contain a volume of water between five and seven times that of the Amazon River.

> **THE REYNISDRANGAR 'NEEDLES'**
>
> Sea stacks are erosion features formed by wave action. The distinctive Reynisdrangar 'Needles' near Vík are some of Iceland's best examples of stacks. The highest of the stacks rises over 66m (216ft) above sea level. Legend has it that they were formed one night when two trolls were trying to drag a three-masted ship ashore. When daylight broke it was revealed that the ship had turned to stone.

SOUTH ICELAND

▲ *Above: View south from the Mýrdalsjökull icecap to the coastal lowlands.*
▶▶ *Opposite: A distant view of the volcano Hekla. It has erupted frequently over historic time.*

THE REDOUBTABLE KATLA

Just as Vatnajökull has its subglacial volcano Grimsvötn, so **Mýrdalsjökull** has the equally dangerous Katla (or cauldron). This sleeping giant has probably erupted 20 times since Iceland was first settled. When Katla is active, the ice melts rapidly, forming a subglacial lake which eventually finds its way to the surface. The result is a devastating glacial burst, or *jökulhlaup*. The most serious of these are said to have a volume of water five times the flow of the Amazon. Over the years the glacial bursts have built up the vast Mýrdalssandur south of the icecap. Katla erupts every 40–80 years and with the last eruption in 1918, another volcanic event is overdue!

In early 2010 another Icelandic volcano, **Eyjafjallajökull**, became world news. Its eruption caused a cloud of ash to rise to over 20,000ft, while blasts carried finer material up into the North Atlantic jet stream. For several days the airlines of northern Europe were grounded, causing misery to thousands of stranded passengers. Ironically, the volcano revived Iceland's tourist industry and it is estimated that over 100,000 people came to see the spectacular eruptions. At the time of writing, Eyjafjallajökull, although still erupting, has quietened down. But there is a bigger concern. This volcano has erupted three times since the Vikings settled here in the 9th century. On each occasion it has been followed within a year by the eruption of Katla – a much more dangerous volcano capable of causing flooding.

To the north of Mýrdalsjökull and immediately east of Hekla lies the **Landmannalaugar** area, famed for the variable colours in the rhyolite rocks.

The Skógar Area ★★

The small settlement of **Skógar**, nestling beneath the Mýrdalsjökull icecap, makes a good centre from which to explore the area. Just east of the village is the short glacial **Jökulsá River**, which is often called the Fúlilækur, or 'foul river'. The stench is caused by large quantities of sulphur which the river washes down from Katla. The main attraction in Skógar itself is the **Folk Museum**, which is located in a complex of turf farmhouses that have been reassembled on the site. The museum has over 6000 artefacts reflecting life in southern Iceland over the centuries. It is open from Jun–Aug daily 09:00–18:00, May and Sep daily 10:00–17:00, Oct–Apr daily 11:00–16:00, tel: 487 8845. Skógar's other attraction is one of Iceland's highest waterfalls, **Skógafoss**, where, just west of the village, the river Skóga drops 60m (197ft) into a narrow gorge. Further west is another waterfall worth visiting. This is **Seljalandsfoss**. It is possible to take the path behind the falls, although a change in wind direction can make this a drenching experience.

The West of the Region ★★★

There are two modern settlements located in the west of southern Iceland. **Hella** has developed in recent years as a market town, but has little to interest the tourist. **Hvolsvöllur**, to the east, is another market town which has a good view of snow-capped Hekla to the north. The Hvolsvöllur area has numerous associations with the *Njáls Saga* and guided tours to the main sites can be arranged from the town.

THE INTERIOR

Although one of the most seductive parts of the country, the interior of Iceland has a very limited access. It is only open to traffic from late June to the end of August, and even during this period four-wheel-drive vehicles are essential. Even during the summer months, bad weather can descend very rapidly and roads can become impassable. The interior is, neverthe-less, a part of Iceland which all visitors should experience if at all possible. It has been described as one of Europe's last wilderness areas, and travellers should be aware that there are few services available – no accommoda-tion, no petrol stations, no restaurants and, in places, not even a road! For informa-tion on conditions contact Iceland Road and Coastal Administration, tel: 522 1000 or www.vegagerdin.is

> **FOLLOWING THE NJÁLS SAGA**
>
> The most popular and blood-thirsty of the Sagas is certainly the *Njáls Saga*, the setting for which was the land to the north of **Hvolsvöllur**. The story includes characters such as Hallgeður Longlegs, Gissur the White, and various members of the Njál family. The Saga features murder, arson, betrayal, love, and a continuous family feud – indeed, an ancient version of a modern-day soap opera! Archaeological digs in the 20th century suggest that much of the story may be true. Visitors can go to the **Saga Centre** in Hvolsvöllur, and guided tours are available to the sites mentioned in the *Njáls Saga*. Open mid-May–mid-Sep, daily 09:00–18:00, tel: 487 8138. The Centre also offers a 3-5 hour tour around the most important saga sites – ask for details.

SOUTH ICELAND

Crossing Rivers in the Interior

One of the main hazards when driving across the interior of Iceland is the number of rivers which have to be crossed. Even with high-clearance four-wheel-drive vehicles, this exercise is fraught with danger. One of the main problems is the variable climate and its effect on river volume. Some of the river flows are dominated by rainfall, which has an immediate effect. Other rivers are fed by melting snows, which means that they may very well be at their peak volume on a sunny day. The best advice to drivers is to travel in convoy, and check on the river and weather conditions carefully before attempting a crossing. For information on conditions, telephone Public Administration on 563 1500.

Kjölur Route

Most of the routes start in the southwest and end up in the north near Akureyri, Sauðarkrókur or Mývatn. The **Kjölur Route** runs northeast from the Gullfoss area and passes over the Central Highland desert, the track rising to over 700m (2300ft) between the Langjökull and Hofsjökull icecaps. It also passes the Hveravellir geothermal area, with its fumeroles and hot springs, before dropping down to meet the northern arm of the Ring Road near Blönduós. Although it is the easiest of the routes through the interior, it was unpopular for many centuries as it was often the haunt of bandits.

Sprengisandur Route

The alternative **Sprengisandur Route** initially follows the valley of the Þjórsá River before crossing the pass at around 800m (2625ft) between the Hofsjökull and the smaller Tungnafellsjökull icecaps. It then follows the Skjálfandafljót valley northwards to join the Ring Road near Goðafoss. This is a more difficult and hostile route, but gives some superb views of the icecaps.

Hekla and Haiföss

A less adventurous, but equally exciting, day trip takes road No. 26 which becomes gravel before reaching an information site and excellent viewpoint of Hekla. From here Landmannalaugar can be visited, while a short alternative trip visits Haiföss, a pair of waterfalls formed by the same river which are Iceland's highest and which fall into a vast canyon.

▶ *Right: A super jeep with enlarged wheels crosses a river in spate in central Iceland.*

BEST TIME TO VISIT

June–September has the best weather, but rain can be expected all year, with deep snowfalls on the higher land. On weekends in July–August popular spots like Skaftafell can become uncomfortably crowded. The interior is rarely open for tourists before late June. Winter snows begin again by mid-September.

GETTING THERE

BSÍ buses on the Reykjavík–Höfn service use the southern arm of the Ring Road and stop at the main tourist 'honeypots'. There are no internal airports in the region, although there are a few private airstrips. **Strætó** run buses along the south coast from Reykjavík as far as Höfn. *See* p59 for contact details.

GETTING AROUND

Service buses using the Ring Road are few and far between and visitors on a budget may find it more convenient to hitch lifts in summer when the roads are busy. A private car is most convenient. This is also true of travelling in the interior, where four-wheel-drive is essential.

WHERE TO STAY

There is nothing in the luxury classification in south Iceland, but plenty of mid-range choices although these fill up rapidly in the height of the season.

Mid-range

The **Edda Group** have summer hotels at Skógar and Vík, tel: 444 4000 (main booking centre).

Hótel Hvolsvöllur, Hlíðarvegur 7, 860 Hvolsvöllur, tel: 487 8050, www.hotelhvolsvollur.is
Icelandair Hotel Klaustur, Klausturvegur 6, Kirkjubæjar-klaustur, tel: 487 4900, www.hotelklaustur.com Beautifully sited. Quiet and very friendly.
Hótel Skaftafell, Skaftafelli 2, Freysnesi, 785 Öræfi, tel: 478 1945, www.hotelskaftafell.is At the heart of the National Park.

Budget

Guesthouse Ásgarður, Hvols-völlur, tel: 487 1440, www.asgardurinn.is Guesthouse and sleeping bag accommodation.

Farmhouse accommodation, for details and booking, tel: 575 6700. There are **Youth Hostels** at **Fljótsdalur**, near Hvolsvöllur, at **Reynisbrekka**, outside Vík, and at **Vagnsstaðir**, west of Höfn. Booking, tel: 575 6700.

Camping

Official camp sites in the area have excellent facilities. The more popular ones, such as in the Skaftafell National Park, can become very crowded on weekends in the summer.

WHERE TO EAT

Good restaurants are rather hard to find. The best bets are dining rooms of larger hotels, though they may be expensive.

Snack bars at petrol stations are good value and offer a wholesome tourist menu.

TOURS AND EXCURSIONS

Most excursions here involve the icecaps of Vatnajökull and Mýrdalsjökull. Many of these can be booked in Reykjavík with firms such as Reykjavík Excursions (tel: 580 5400) or BSÍ. Local firms run snowmobile and glacier buggy tours on the icecaps. **Vatnajökull Tours**, Vagnsstaðir, 781 Suðursveit, tel: 478 1000/894 3133 offer Glacier Jeep tours to Vatnajökull. **Zodiac** boat trips are available on Jökulsárlón. Ask at the shop/café or tel: 860 9996, icelagoon.com From close to the Hótel Skaftafell excursions are run by tractor and trailer across the shallow sea to Ingólfshöfði where there are views of puffins and other seabirds and a magnificent view back to Vatnajökull, tel: 894 0894, www.localguide.is

USEFUL CONTACTS

There are several **Tourist Information Centres** in the area. The largest centre is in the **Skaftafell NationalPark**, tel: 470 8300. Others are at **Skógar**, tel: 487 8843; **Kirkjubæjarklaustur**, tel: 487 4620; **Vík**, tel: 487 1395; **Hvolsvöllur** and **Hella**, tel: 487 8043.

VÍK	J	F	M	A	M	J	J	A	S	O	N	D
AVE. TEMP. °C	-0.4	0.2	0.7	3.2	6.5	9.4	11.2	10.4	7.5	4.5	1.1	-0.4
AVE. TEMP. °F	31.3	32.4	33.3	37.8	43.7	48.9	52.2	50.7	45.5	40.1	34	31.3
AVE. RAINFALL mm	145	130	130	115	118	131	121	159	141	185	137	133
AVE. RAINFALL in	5.71	5.12	5.12	4.53	4.65	5.16	4.77	6.26	5.55	7.29	5.39	5.24

8
The Westman Islands

The *Vestmannaeyjar*, or Westman Islands, are a group of 15 islands and rock skerries some 11km (7 miles) off the southern coast of Iceland. Only one, the largest, known as **Heimaey** (pronounced *hay may*), is inhabited. The islands are located on the Mid-Atlantic Ridge and are of recent geological origin. They were formed of volcanic material, spewed out of submarine volcanoes between 8000 and 3000BC. This process has continued into the 20th century with the formation of the new island of **Surtsey**, created by an eruption which lasted for four years, between 1963 and 1967. The eruption was seen on television screens around the world, and scientific studies of the volcano have continued to this day. Ten years later, an eruption occurred on Heimaey, which forced the evacuation of the entire population, fortunately without loss of life. After this new volcano, named **Eldfell**, had quietened down, the inhabitants returned to find that the island had grown in size by 15% and that the lava flow had improved the shelter around the harbour.

A Violent History

The history of the Westman Islands has been typified by violence and tragedy. The islands were first inhabited by a group of **Irish slaves** (these 'Westmen' may have given the islands their name) intent on escape after murdering their master, Hjörleifur Hróðmarsson, the foster brother of Ingólfur Arnarson, in turn recognized as the first genuine Icelandic settler. When Ingólfur heard the news, he quickly tracked

DON'T MISS

** **Þjóðhátíð:** the Westman Islands' National Day held on the first weekend in August.
* **Heimaey's volcanoes:** easy hiking trails over both the old and new volcanoes of Helgafell and Eldfell.
* **The Aquarium:** at Heimaey's Natural History Museum, with several rare North Atlantic fish.
* **Sea-bird cliffs:** on the north of Heimaey and also on other islands, with thousands of puffins.

◄ *Opposite: The sea cliffs of Heimaey, famous for their nesting puffins.*

THE WESTMAN ISLANDS

CLIMATE

The Westman Islands' maritime position has the effect of moderating the climate, making it milder than that of Reykjavík in winter, but cooler in summer. **Rainfall** is high, with an annual total of 1713mm (67.5in). Average temperatures in **January** stay above freezing, and any snowfall is light. The average **July** temperature is 9.6°C (49°F), which is lower than that of the mainland. Fog and low cloud are common.

▼ *Below: The town of Heimaey has frequently been threatened by volcanic activity. The last lava flow in 1973 destroyed some of the houses but actually improved the harbour.*

down the slaves and killed them. The very first permanent settler in the Westman Islands, probably around 900, is believed to have been **Herjólfur Barðursson**, who was looking for a peaceful escape from the feuding on the mainland. The first church was built around 1000, and shortly afterwards the islands were purchased by the **Bishops of Skálholt**. Later British traders took over the islands as their headquarters in the North Atlantic until they were driven out by the Danes in the mid-16th century.

In 1627 the Westman Islands were attacked by a group of **North African pirates**, who murdered over 40 people and took away around 250 hostages, most of whom were sold as slaves in the markets of Morocco. By this time the Bishops of Skálholt had turned the islands over to the King of Norway. The succeeding centuries saw further tragedies – disease, starvation, scurvy and dysentry. The **Laki eruptions** in 1783 and the subsequent 'haze fires' killed most of the livestock and poisoned the sea. The 20th century saw a change in fortunes, with the development of the fishing industry, but a further setback came in 1973 with the **eruption of Eldfell**. After the evacuation of Heimaey, many of the inhabitants, who returned to find their houses destroyed by lava, decided to emigrate to other countries.

Today, the Westman Islands are thriving. Prosperity is based almost entirely on the **fishing** industry and the majority of the 5300 residents are involved in fishing or tourism. The first freezing plant was installed in 1908 and shortly afterwards the islands were connected with the mainland by submarine electricity and telephone cables and a freshwater pipeline. The Westman Islands have a fishing fleet of over 100 vessels, which account for around 15% of Iceland's total exports. The main fish caught are sole, cod, halibut and haddock. There are also salmon farms which are located in the outer harbour. Some of the fish is exported fresh, but the majority is processed on Heimaey.

HEIMAEY ★★

The only inhabited island in *Vestmannaeyjar* is **Heimaey** (the 'home island'). The other islands are too steep-sided for harbours, although some are used for summer sheep pastures. The town of Heimaey, with a population of just over 4000, is attractively located around the **harbour** and stretches southward to cover about a third of the island. To the north of the town are some sheer cliffs, while to the south the lava flow from the 1973 eruption has contrived to make a sheltered entrance to the harbour. Look out for the **mural** on the side of one of the buildings near the harbour. It was painted by local schoolchildren and depicts the town on the morning of the 1973 eruption. Forming the southeastern background to the town are the two low volcanic peaks of **Helgafell** and the more recent **Eldfell**.

◀ *Left: View of Heimaey harbour. The port accounts for 15% of Iceland's fish exporting business.*

ÞJÓÐHÁTÍÐ

The main social event of the Westman Islands' calendar is their annual **National Day** held over the first weekend in August. It began in 1874, when bad weather prevented the islanders from reaching the mainland to celebrate Iceland's National Day. They therefore decided to hold their own festival a month later, and this has now become an annual tradition. The festivities take place in a large valley called **Herjólfsdalur**, which becomes a huge camp site for the occasion. It is the location for singing, dancing, much drinking and a large bonfire. Some mainland critics disapprove, suggesting that the festival has become a mere showpiece for supporters of Vestmannæyjar independence. Nevertheless, it is hugely enjoyed by both islanders and those who come over from the mainland to join in the celebrations.

THE WESTMAN ISLANDS

▲ *Above: An aerial view of Heimaey harbour.*
▶ *Opposite: Eldfell rises to 205m (673ft) and can be climbed from Heimaey town.*

Visitors arrive at Heimaey by air or ferry, and there is enough to see here to make a two- or three-day stay worthwhile. Despite the existence of coaches and taxis, most of the island can be covered **on foot**.

Museums ★★★

Heimaey's **Aquarium and Natural History Museum**, at Heiðarvegur 12, was established in 1964. It has the usual selection of geological specimens and stuffed birds, but the highlight is the aquarium, which has a wonderful collection of Icelandic fish, both common and rare, plus a live video link to a puffin colony. Open mid-May–mid-Sep daily 11:00–17:00, mid-Sep–mid-May Sat 13:00–16:00, tel: 481 1997.

The **Folk Museum** is located above the library. This museum combines an art gallery with a collection of stamps, currency and historic household artefacts. Open mid-May–mid-Sep daily 11:00–17:00, mid-Sep–mid-May Sat 13:00–16:00, tel: 488 2045. **Eldheimar** is a remembrance museum of the 1973 eruption and includes the recently excavated house

SURTSEY

In November 1963 a new volcano rose from the sea bed about 18km (11 miles) southwest of Heimaey. This was named **Surtsey** after the legendary Norse giant **Surtur**. The eruptions lasted for four years, and at their peak sent up a column of steam and ash over 10,000m (33,000ft) into the sky. When the activity calmed down, Surtsey had reached a height of 150m (492ft) and covered an area of 3km² (1.2 sq miles). Thereafter Surtsey became a natural laboratory for scientists, who have observed its gradual colonization by insects, birds, plants, and mammals such as seals. Surtsey is still off limits to visitors, but it is possible to fly over the dormant volcano in a chartered light aircraft.

at Gerðisbraut 10 which was buried for 40 years under ash and lava, forcing the evacuation of a family with three young children. There is also a film of the 1963 eruption during which Surtsey was born. Open April–mid-Oct daily 11:00–18:00, mid-Oct–Mar Wed–Sun 13:00–17:00, tel: 488 2702, eldheimar.is

Other Points of Interest ★★★

Heimaey's modern white **church** is worth a look. Opposite the entrance is a memorial to lost fishermen. An older stone church, the **Landakirkja**, dates from 1788. It has an unusual interior arrangement, in that the pulpit is placed immediately behind the altar. For information on the opening times of the Landakirkja ask at the TIC. The most recent **lava flows** are readily accessible and give good views over the harbour and also towards the mainland, where the Vatnajökull and Mýrdalsjökull icecaps can be seen on a clear day. **Eldfell**, which rises to 205m (673ft), can quite easily be climbed on the pathways, some with artificial steps, leading up to the crater rim. There are still plenty of hot cinders and fumeroles, so stout footwear is recommended. Be prepared, too, for the stench of sulphur. The slightly higher **Helgafell** can also be climbed. This was formed about 5000 years ago and rises to a height of 226m (742ft). Take the path from the end of the football pitch.

HEIMAEY'S LATEST VOLCANIC EPISODE

In January 1973 a serious volcanic eruption occurred on the eastern side of the island of Heimaey. The fishing fleet were able to evacuate the entire population of 5300 people. A massive amount of lava and ash threatened the town, demolishing houses and causing fires. The greatest danger was that the lava flow, which was 165m (540ft) high, would block the harbour entrance. Without the harbour, the evacuation of Heimaey would have been permanent. The flow was eventually stopped by spraying it with millions of gallons of sea water. The island had increased in size by 15% and over half the town had been destroyed. The good news was that the lava flow actually protected the harbour entrance, while the high underground temperatures provided the island with hot water and heating.

THE WESTMAN ISLANDS

Boat Trips from Heimaey ★★★

There are a number of boat trips from Heimaey. The tours usually pass the salmon farms, the pen where Keiko the killer whale resided for a number of years (*see* panel, page 12), and the sea-bird cliffs. On calm days, the boats go right in amongst the caves and stacks along the coast. Sea-fishing and whale-watching trips are also available.

Sport ★★★

The Westman Islands have what is arguably Iceland's best 18-hole **golf course**, located in Herjólfsdalur. It is the country's most southerly golf course, and the mild climate that generally prevails in this part of the country means that it is playable for much of the year. There is also a superb **indoor swimming pool**, complete with sauna, jacuzzi, solarium and gym. There are also several opportunities to rent horses.

BIRD-WATCHING ON THE WESTMAN ISLANDS

The Westman Islands form one of the prime sea-bird haunts in Northern Europe. Several spectacular cliffs (particularly on northern Heimaey) and rich food in the sea have led to quite amazing numbers of nesting sea birds. The islands support Iceland's only breeding colonies of manx shearwater, Leach's petrel and storm petrel. However, as these birds are largely nocturnal in their habits, observation is difficult. There are vast numbers of **gannets**, particularly on the smaller outer islands. Other species include five types of auk, fulmars and gulls. By far the most common sea bird, however, is the **puffin**, with literally hundreds of thousands of nesting pairs. Though the puffin was once part of the staple diet of the Westman Islanders, human predation never seemed to affect the numbers of this endearing bird.

▼ *Below: Too cute to eat? Puffin is still a delicacy in the Westman Islands.*

BEST TIME TO VISIT

Snowfall is low in winter, but rain and mist occur year-round. July and August are warmest. National Day (in August) is a good time to visit.

GETTING THERE

The **ferry** Herjólfur runs from Landeyjahöfn to Vestmannaeyjar. The trip takes approximately 30 minutes on rough seas. The Herjólfur is run by Eimskip, tel: 481 2800, eimskip.is The ferry Norröna, run by the Faeroese Smyril Line (tel: 298 345 900, www.smyril-line.com) all year linking Iceland with Esbjerg in Denmark, Bergen in Norway, Tórshavn in the Faroe Islands, and Shetland. Ernir (Eagle Air) currently has two **flights** daily from Reykjavík domestic airport, tel: 562 4200/562 2640, eagleair.ferdathing.is No direct flights to Akureyri.

GETTING AROUND

Most of Heimaey can easily be seen on foot as it covers only 13.4km² (5.2 sq miles). For local **taxis**, tel: 481 2038. **Car hire** is available at the airport (Hertz, tel: 522 4400).

WHERE TO STAY

Mid-range

Hótel Vestmanaeyjar, Vestmannabraut 28, tel: 481 2900, fax: 481 1696, hotel vestmannaeyjar.is Heimaey's best hotel. Can arrange horse riding, sea fishing and bike hire.

Hótel Eyjar, Bárustíg 2, tel: 481 3636, hoteleyjar.is Offers both apartments and rooms.

Budget

Gistiheimilið Árný, Illugagata 7, 900 Vestmannaeyjar, tel /fax: 481 2082. Near pool. Cooking facilities available.

Gistíheimilið Hamar, Herjólfs-götu 4, tel: 481 3400. Comfortable and conveniently located.

Gistiheimilið Sunnuhóll, Vestmannabraut 25, 900 Vestmannaeyjar, tel: 481 2900, fax: 481 1696. Comfortable guesthouse near the harbour.

Gistiheimilið Hreiðrið, Faxastígur 33, 900 Vestmannaeyjar, tel: 481 1045, fax: 481 1414. Good wheelchair access. Best budget option.

Faxi Youth Hostel, Faxastígur 38, 900 Vestmannaeyjar, tel: 481 2915, fax: 481 1497. Open Jun–Sep. Book in advance.

Camping

The **Heimaey camp site** at Herjólfsdalur, tel: 481 2922, has good facilities.

WHERE TO EAT

Heimaey has a wide variety of eating places to suit all pockets. Hotel restaurants are generally the best, though also the most expensive. The **Einsi Kaldi** in the Hótel Vestmanaeyjar is excellent, but not cheap.

Slippurinn, Strandvegur, tel: 481 1515. Remodelled work-shop that once serviced the islands' fishing fleet. Fish and Scandinavian dishes.

Gott, Báristígur 11, tel: 481 3060. The owners are best-selling authors of cook books and prepare everything fresh each day. For cheap pizzas, try **Pizza 67**, Heiðarvegur 5, tel: 481 1567.

TOURS AND EXCURSIONS

Viking Tours, Tanagata 7, tel: 488 4884 offers daily **coach and boat sightseeing tours** of the islands (including Surtsey), as well as **sea angling and whale watching trips**. Ribsafari, tel: 661 1810 offer **rigid inflatable boats (RIB) tours** to see whales and birdlife. There are also several other boat trip operators. Eyjamyndir, Faxastíg 33, tel: 481 1414 offer guided **hiking trips** for individuals and groups, exploring the lava fields, and the cliffs to see the puffins.

USEFUL CONTACTS

Tourist Information Centre, Bárustígur 2, tel: 488 2555, www.vestmannaeyjar.is Also a Tourist Information Centre in the Folk Museum, open weekdays 10:00–18:00, weekends 11:00–17:00, closed Sun in winter, tel: 481 3555. **Town Hall**, Kirkjuveg 50, Vestmann-aeyjabær, tel: 488 2000 has information on the islands, accommodation, activities etc.

HEIMAEY	J	F	M	A	M	J	J	A	S	O	N	D
AVE. TEMP.°C	1.3	2.0	1.7	3.4	5.6	8.0	9.8	9.6	7.4	5.0	2.4	1.4
AVE. TEMP.°F	34.3	35.6	35.1	38.1	42.1	46.4	49.6	49.3	45.3	41.0	36.3	34.5
AVE. RAINFALL mm	158	139	141	117	105	102	95	140	131	162	154	143
AVE. RAINFALL in	6.23	5.48	5.55	4.61	4.14	4.02	3.74	5.52	5.16	6.38	6.07	5.63

Travel Tips

Tourist Information

Limited information is available at the Icelandic Embassy, 2A Hans Street, London, SW1X 0JE, tel: 0207 259 3999. The official **Visit Iceland Official Tourism Information Site**, www.ice tourist.is is very useful. There is also a website specific to Reykjavík – www.visitreykjavik. is The main office in Iceland is the **Tourist Information Centre**, Aðalstræti 2, Reykjavík, tel: 590 1550. Open Jun–mid-Sep daily 08:30–19:00, mid-Sep–May weekdays 09:00–18:00, Sat 09:00–16:00, Sun 09:00–14:00. **Icelandic Travel Market**, Bankastræti 2, tel: 562 3045, is useful for information on tours/excursions etc.

Entry Requirements

A valid passport is required for all visitors, except those from Nordic countries, who only need an identity card. Visas are needed for visitors from certain countries, which do not include Canada, USA, the EU, Australia and many others. If in doubt, ask at an Icelandic embassy or consulate before departure. An entry stamp in a passport is valid for 3 months.

Customs

Visitors over the age of 20 may bring in free of duty: 1 litre spirits + 1 litre wine + 6 litres beer OR 3 litres wine + 5 litres beer OR 1 litre spirits + 9 litres beer OR 1.5 litres wine + 9 litres beer OR 12 litres beer and 200 cigarettes OR 250g other tobacco products (minimum age 18 years). The duty-free shop at Keflavík Airport (in the baggage reclaim hall) is open to arriving passengers and in view of the high cost of living in Iceland, it is advisable to make use of this. There are restrictions on most meat and dairy products, but visitors may bring in up to 10kg of other foods. Icelandic VAT is high. Much of this can be refunded on leaving, at various places in Reykjavík and at the airport. The former is better as the airport office may be closed (it keeps 'shop hours' not 'flight hours').

Health Requirements

Iceland has no specific health problems and inoculations are unnecessary. All health services are publicly provided and free for citizens of Nordic and EU countries (bring EU Health Card). Dental services are privately provided and costs are on par with Europe and the USA.

Getting There

By Air: The main airline serving Iceland is the national carrier **Icelandair** (tel: 505 0100, www. icelandair.com), with services from Amsterdam, Baltimore, Barcelona, Bergen, Boston, Chicago, Copenhagen, Detroit, Faroe Islands, Frankfurt, Glasgow, Gothenburg, Helsinki, London, Luxembourg, Milan, New York, Orlando, Paris, Salzburg, Stockholm and Washington DC. Icelandair offers passengers travelling between Europe and USA a stopover deal for up to 72 hours. **SAS** flies from Copenhagen, Oslo and Stockholm. **WOW** flies to Keflavík from London Gatwick and also from many other European cities, tel: 0118 321 8384, www.wowair.co.uk **EasyJet** offers flights from Belfast, Bristol, Edinburgh, London Gatwick, London Luton and Manchester, and from Basel-Mulhouse-Freiburg and Geneva in Switzerland. All incoming international flights land at **Keflavík** Airport (tel: 425 6010), 50km (31 miles) from Reykjavík. Regular non-stop Fly Bus coaches run from the airport to the capital, taking 45 minutes. The city terminal is at the City Bus Station; however the bus also calls at some hotels in the city.

By Sea: The Faroes shipping company **Smyril Line**, tel: 472 1111, runs a car ferry service to Iceland throughout the year. The trip links Hirtshals, Denmark to Tórshavn (Faroes) and Seyðisfjorður. The schedule is variable, so consult www.

smyrilline.com which posts the annual schedule. The *MS Norröna* accommodates some 1000 passengers and 250 cars. The ferry arrives in Seyðisfjörður, which is over 700km (435 miles) from Reykjavík along the northern or southern routes of the Ring Road.

WHAT TO PACK

The unpredictable weather means that visitors should be prepared for anything. Wind and rain can be incessant, so water- and windproof jacket and trousers are essential. Sweater, scarf, hat and gloves are also advisable. A pair of hiking boots are necessary, even on a coach tour, as most of the sites involve a walk, often over rough ground. Bring a swimsuit for the geothermally heated swimming pools. Formal clothes are necessary in quality hotels and restaurants. The light provides marvellous conditions for photography. Binoculars are essential for observing wildlife.

MONEY MATTERS

Icelandic currency is the **króna** (Ikr), divided into 100 aurar. Notes come in denominations of 5000 Ikr, 2000 Ikr, 1000 Ikr and 500 Ikr, and coins in 100 Ikr, 50 Ikr, 10 Ikr, 5 Ikr and Ikr. Currency may be bought abroad (sometimes with difficulty), but the local exchange rate is better. There are four **banks** in Iceland – Arion Bank, Íslandsbanki, Landsbankinn and MP Bank – usually open 09:15–16:00, Mon–Fri; opening hours may be erratic in rural areas. There are exchange facilities at Keflavík

Airport from 06:30–18:30. **Travellers cheques** may be cashed at most hotels. **ATMs** are common in Reykjavík and other towns and are increasingly found in rural areas. **Credit cards** can be used to obtain cash from banks and are widely accepted in hotels, shops and restaurants, but not always at petrol service stations. **VAT** on most purchases is currently at 25.5%.

ACCOMMODATION

Prices are high, particularly in **hotels**. Reykjavík and Akureyri have international-standard hotels offering *en-suite* bathrooms, restaurants, shops and often indoor pools. Tourist-class hotels throughout the country offer fewer facilities, but most have a restaurant and rooms with a private shower and toilet. A unique Icelandic feature is the **summer hotel**. These open for June and August but for the rest of the year they are boarding schools and colleges. Facilities vary: some offer only **sleeping-bag accommodation**, while others also have restaurants and pools. Most common budget accommodation is the **guesthouse**. Located throughout the country, they usually offer bed and breakfast. A list of hotels and guesthouses can be obtained from tourist information centres. Advance booking is advisable during peak season. **Farmhouse accommodation** (tel: 570 2700, www.farmholidays.is) is widely offered by Icelandic farmers, usually on a bed and breakfast or sleeping-bag arrangement. Some farms

provide self-catering cottages, others have horses and boats for rent. **Youth hostels** are economical and there are around 30 in the country. Most close in the winter. They usually offer sleeping-bag accommodation and cooking facilities, though some provide family rooms and meals. Pre-booking is essential in July and August. Contact Hostelling International Icelandic, which has 32 hostels around the country, tel: 575 6700, www.hostel.is Despite the weather, **camping** is very popular. There are over 100 sites, often in national parks or scenic areas. Facilities vary – some are quite primitive, others have toilets, showers, snack bars, kitchens and pools. Note that facilities may not be on the site but in the nearest settlement. When camping in non-designated areas, obtain the land-

PUBLIC HOLIDAYS

New Year's Day • 1 January
Easter • Maundy Thursday, Good Friday, Easter Sunday, Easter Monday
First Day of Summer • Third Tuesday in April
Labour Day • 1 May
Ascension Day • May/June
Seamen's Day • Early June
Independence Day • 17 June
August Public Holiday • First Weekend in August
Rettir • September (sheep and horse round-ups in rural areas)
Christmas Eve • 24 December
Christmas Day • 25 December
Boxing Day • 26 December
New Year's Eve • 31 December

owner's permission. Because of possible wind and rain, tents should be durable. A booklet, *Camping in Iceland*, (obtainable from all tourist information centres) has a list of officially designated sites. Hikers in remote areas can make use of **mountain huts**, which usually have only basic facilities.

USEFUL WORDS AND PHRASES

Yes, No • Já, Nei
Hello • Góðen dag
Goodbye • Bless
Thank you • Takk fyrir
How are you? • Hvad sergirdu gott?
Toilet • Snyrting
Ladies, Gents • Konur, Karlar
How much is it? • Hvad kostar petta?
Airport • Flúgvöllur
Ferry • Ferja
My name is • Ég heiti
I don't understand • Ég skil ekki
Guesthouse • Gistheimili
Open • Opið
Closed • Lokað
Beer • Bjór
Bread • Brauð
Coffee • Kaffi
Milk • Mjólk
Tea • Te
Water • Vatn
Days of the week:
Sunnudagur, Mánudagur,
Priðjudagur, Miðvikudagur,
Fimmtudagur, Fostudagur,
Laugardagur
Some numbers:
0 • null   1 • einn
2 • tveir   3 • prír
4 • fjórir   5 • fimm
6 • sex   7 • sjö
8 • átta   9 • níu
10 • tíu
100 • hundrad
1000 • thúsund

They are owned by the Touring Club of Iceland, tel: 568 2533, who charge a small fee for their use.

EATING OUT

Food is a major expense. With a service charge, plus alcohol, the bill may be double that which tourists would pay at home. There are plenty of **restaurants** in Reykjavík and to a lesser extent in Akureyri, but elsewhere they are mainly confined to hotels. Reykjavík has a range of ethnic restaurants, including Japanese, Indian, Thai, Italian and Chinese. Cheaper are the American fast-food chains, pizza restaurants and hot dogs stalls. In rural areas, cafés attached to service stations offer cheap, filling food, usually with a daily 'special'. In summer, look for the sign 'Tourist Menu' – this is usually soup, a main course and coffee for a set price. **Alcohol** is very expensive and can only be bought by those over 20, from State Monopoly Shops which have limited opening hours. The traditional Icelandic tipple is *brennivin*, a schnapps made from potatoes and flavoured with caraway. The main brand is Svarti Dauði, which means 'Black Death'!

TRANSPORT

Iceland has no railways, so travel is mainly by road and air. **Air**: Difficult surface conditions, particularly in winter, mean that flights are a common way to get around. Most routes are operated by Icelandair's subsidiary Air Iceland. Various bargain air passes are available, including Holiday Air Rover, offering round routing from Reykjavík via Akureyri, Egilsstaðir, Höfn, Ísafjörður and back to Reykjavík. The main centre for domestic flights is the Reykjavík Domestic Airport.

Road: Iceland has a good network of roads, including Road No. 1, the so-called Ring Road, completed in 1974. About 80% of the Ring Road is metalled, the rest gravel. During dry periods, the gravel roads can be dusty, and flying stones can damage cars. Tracks through the interior are usually open only in July and August and involve fording rivers, so four-wheel-drive vehicles are essential. Petrol is expensive, though diesel is relatively cheap. Driving is on the right and seat belts are obligatory. Headlights must remain on. Speed limits are 50km/h (30 mph) in urban areas, 80km/h (50 mph) outside towns. Look out for sheep in rural areas. Drunk driving regulations are strictly enforced and the legal limit is low. Drivers bringing their own cars need a driving licence, registration document and green card. The Icelandic motoring organization (FÍB) will be allied to home organizations. Filling stations in Reykjavík are open until 23:30; earlier in other parts.

Car Hire: Most international car-hire companies, like Avis, Hertz and Budget are based in Reykjavík. Car hire is expensive, mainly due to the 25.5% VAT. If you plan to go off the metalled roads, a 4WD vehicle is recommended. Minimum age for car hire is 21 for saloon cars and

25 for an off-road vehicle. There is a high demand for car hire in summer and pre-booking is advisable.

Buses: A network of long-distance bus routes covering all the inhabited areas is co-ordinated by BSÍ, based at the main bus terminal in Reykjavík (tel: 562 1011, www.bsi.is). Discount passes, like the Full Circle Pass, allow a complete circuit of the Ring Road (route No. 1) in either direction with as many stops as required. Included in the price are 10% discounts on accommodation and ferries. There is also a pass which allows access to the West Fjords including the ferry from Stykkishólmur to Brjánslækur. There is also a fly/bus pass which allows travel by bus in one direction and a flight back. The Omnibus Pass, which can be bought for 1, 2, 3 or 4 weeks, allows unlimited travel on any bus route for a week and discounts on accommodation. These passes are all offered by BSÍ.

Taxis: Available in the main settlements, taxis are usually driver-owned but the fares are uniform and you pay what is on the meter. Fares are comparable to those in the USA and most European countries. You can also hire taxis for a flat rate to visit places of interest.

Ferries: Car ferries – Landeyjahöfn to Heimaey, Stykkishólmur to Brjánslækur, stopping at Flatey island en route. There is also a ferry from Akureyri to Dalvík to Grímsey, and return, but it does not take vehicles. It operates twice weekly in summer and takes about 7 hours (round trip).

Maps: The Globetrotter Travel Map of Iceland is excellent. Free maps are available in tourist offices and hotels. The Ferdakort map (1:500,000) is good, but expensive. Maps are available the Eymundsson bookshops (Austurstræti 18 and Skóla-vörðustígur 11) and Mál og Menning, Laugavegur 18.

BUSINESS HOURS

Offices usually open 09:00–17:00, Mon–Fri. Shops stay open later, but may close on Saturday in summer. Most supermarkets are open daily; also weekends and holidays. Banks open 09:15–16:00, Mon–Fri. Petrol stations open daily 07:00–23:30.

TIPPING

Service is included in prices for hotels, restaurants and taxis. Tipping is not customary.

TIME DIFFERENCE

Iceland is on Greenwich Mean Time (GMT) throughout the year. In summer it is one hour behind British Summer Time.

COMMUNICATIONS

All Icelandic towns have **post offices** and telephone offices – look for the sign *Póstur og Sími* – usually open Mon–Fri, 08:30–17:00. Stamps are available in supermarkets and hotels. Post boxes are red and often found near hotels. Allow 3–5 days for a letter to reach Europe or North America. The telephone system is very efficient. **Telephone booths** are usually in hotels,

restaurants and service stations. Subscribers in the telephone directory are listed by their first names. There are no regional codes; the international code for Iceland is 354. If making international calls from Iceland, dial 00 first then the international code for the country concerned. For the UK dial 44. For Canada and USA, it is 1. Iceland has the highest per capita mobile phone network in the world. GSM is used in the more populated areas and most visitors will be able to use their cell phones, except in more rural areas, when an NMT phone may have to be hired. An option is to buy a SIM card at Keflavík on arrival. These can be topped up if necessary. There are also companies offering SIM cards on the internet which will work in Iceland.

TRAVEL TIPS

Good Reading

Peterson, Mountford (1993) *Birds of Britain and Europe* (Collins).

Hillmarsson, Jóhann Óli, (2000) Icelandic Bird Guide (IÐUNN).

Love, Askell (1983) *The Flora of Iceland* (Almenna Bokafelagid).

Wolesey, Pat (1979) *A Field Key to the Flowering Plants of Iceland* (The Thule Press).

Carwardine, Mark (1986) *Iceland: Nature's Meeting Place* (Iceland Review).

Perkins, John (1983) *Iceland: A Geological Field Guidebook* (Cardiff University).

Magnusson, Magnus (1990) *Iceland Saga* (The Bodley Head).

Sale, Richard (2000, latest update 2014) *The Xenophobe's Guide to Icelanders* (Oval Books).

Internet

Icelanders have enthusiastically adopted information technology. There are a number of Internet cafés in Reykjavík. It is estimated that 96.5% of the population are internet users.

Websites

www.south.is
Travel in south Iceland.

www.travelnet.is
History, geography, culture, accommodations, restaurants, and travel options.

www.iceland.is
Official government website.

www.visiticeland.com
The most comprehensive site for tourists visiting Iceland.

Electricity

Voltage is 220, 50 HZ AC, with two round pin prongs. Visitors may need adapters.

Weights and Measures

Iceland uses the metric system.

Health Precautions

Tap water often smells sulphurous, but is potable all over the country. Food is prepared under stringent health regulations. Visitors in winter should guard against **hypothermia**, while those travelling over snow and ice during summer should use a block to prevent sun and wind burn.

Health Services

The public health service is excellent. There are over 40 hospitals providing 3600 beds. Staff are well trained and are familiar with English. Visitors should have travel insurance to cover unexpected health problems, particularly if planning risky outdoor activities.

Personal Safety

Iceland has one of the lowest crime rates in the world. If it does occur it is usually petty and alcohol-related. Visitors will seldom feel threatened, but should take the usual precautions with money, passports and valuables. The **emergency** telephone number for police and other services is **112**.

Etiquette

Icelanders are very friendly people who welcome all visitors. They are proud of their country and its lack of pollution. Litter is almost nonexistent so please respect this tradition.

Language

Icelandic is a Germanic language and most closely associated with Faroese and Norwegian. It has changed little – Icelanders are still able to read the **Sagas**, written 800 years ago. The alphabet has 32 letters, including a number of extra vowels and consonants. The grammar is extremely complicated. Icelanders try to protect their language from outside influence and develop their own words. Fortunately for visitors, Icelanders are excellent linguists.

Conversion Chart

From	To	Multiply By
Millimetres	Inches	0.0394
Metres	Yards	1.0936
Metres	Feet	3.281
Kilometres	Miles	0.6214
Square kilometres	Square miles	0.386
Hectares	Acres	2.471
Litres	Pints	1.760
Kilograms	Pounds	2.205
Tonnes	Tons	0.984

To convert Celsius to Fahrenheit: x 9 ÷ 5 + 32

INDEX

INDEX